Cruising the Caribbean with Kids

Fun, Facts, and Educational Activities

Nadine Slavinski

Rolling Hitch Press
New York

Contents

Contents

Introduction

The Caribbean is a sailor's dream, with its steady breezes, beautiful islands, and fascinating history. Sailing as a family only makes the experience richer. But where are the best places to sail with kids? How do you keep youngsters occupied on and off the boat? How can you keep kids tuned in to their unique surroundings?

Cruising the Caribbean with Kids is a resource for sailing families of all types, whether your aim is to kick back during a week-long charter, set sail on the adventure of a lifetime, or host the grandkids on your boat during a school vacation. Covering topics from entertainment to education, and from safety to social skills, this book contains tips and tricks for first-time sailors and old hands alike.

This book is divided into three sections. *Part I: Fun* focuses on projects and activities that children can do underway or at anchor. The aim is not just to keep the kids busy but to keep them tuned in to sailing and the cultures, landscapes, and history of the area.

Part II: Facts explores family-friendly destinations in the popular cruising grounds of the Eastern Caribbean and British Virgin Islands, plus a few favorites farther off the beaten track. It's by no means a complete list of the highlights of a huge geographic area, but a great starting point for you to consider when planning your cruise. *Part III; Educational Activities* addresses the common concerns of long-term cruisers, such as schooling and social skills. As a bonus, I've also included an entire unit of study called *The Voyages of Columbus*. This focuses on the great explorer and the impact his discoveries had on both sides of the Atlantic. It is an extended excerpt from my book, *Lesson Plans Ahoy: Hands-On Learning for Sailing Children and Home Schooling Sailors.*

Cruising the Caribbean with Kids is not so much an exhaustive guide as a starting point that will help you launch your cruising dreams. In one hundred concise pages, you'll gain valuable advice on how to make the most of an incredible experience. Many parents love the idea of going sailing as a family but feel apprehensive about setting out. This book will help you overcome those fears and get you on the path to developing your own brand of education and fun. The adventure of a lifetime, for a lifetime awaits!

Part I

FUN

In a perfect world, we'd never need to entertain our kids, because being on a boat among tropical islands would spark a thousand creative pastimes every day. But let's face it: many kids are so accustomed to a stimulation-rich environment that they're not always quick to create their own fun. That's one of the joys of sailing: the chance to unplug from a digital environment, tune in to the real world, and bond as a family. This section suggests various avenues to family fun that will stimulate creativity and make the most of your unique surroundings. Before you know it, you won't need this book or any other: the kids will be making their own fun!

Busy crew, happy crew!

Chapter 1

The Benefits of Extended Travel as a Family

Whether you're taking a week-long Caribbean charter or devoting several seasons to this fascinating part of the world, the experience will stay with your family for a lifetime. The benefits of extended travel as a family can be enormous—especially when the form of travel is as unique as sailing. In this chapter, I identify five of the key benefits of extended travel time and then consider what age is best when it comes to sailing with children.

The Magic of Family Time

Travel allows families to deepen a truly special bond. In normal life, family members usually go their separate ways, but when you're traveling, you're a unit. Ideally, you'll assign each child an area of responsibility and include them in your decision-making. This makes them team members, not passengers.

It's not only children who benefit from family travel. Taking a sailing sabbatical also allowed my overworked husband to re-establish his relationship with our son. They had time for fun, conversation, and shared projects every single day for days on end—a priceless experience! Similarly, siblings learn to depend on one another because a traveling family becomes a team. And while this doesn't always translate to less bickering between siblings, it certainly creates a foundation for solid relationships.

The Gift of Perspective

Another benefit of extended family travel is the perspective it helps children develop. As a teacher, I can always tell which of my students have had more stimulating life experiences. Kids with travel experiences always stand out—especially those who have lived a special kind of adventure such as sailing. These kids know that the world does not run to a calendar hung on the refrigerator back at home. They understand that not everybody lives the same way as in suburb X, Y, or Z. They appreciate how small kindnesses between people of different cultures can go a long way. And they know that "facts" are not always what they seem, whether they appear on a weather forecast, a history book, or the front page of a newspaper.

How do travel experiences manifest themselves in a school setting? Students who have traveled are likely to develop their own interests and viewpoints rather than simply following trends. They can often balance different sides of an issue and take different perspectives. Kids who travel are more likely to seek and appreciate connections between subjects, too. They want to understand things, not just memorize. Schools today put a growing emphasis on developing well-rounded, critical thinkers who can adapt to the challenges of a rapidly changing world. What better way to develop this than through family travel?

Appreciating Limited Resources

Power, water, fuel, money, and even food have to be stocked and monitored carefully when you're on a boat. It's only on land that some of these necessities are available in seemingly endless supply. Children who sail learn to value resources and to make the most of them. They learn to work for what they want or need, whether that means collecting rain water for a shower or solar power for their devices. They witness islanders living lifestyles that are more dependent on ingenuity than consumption. As a consequence, they come to appreciate nature and environmental issues in a way few of their peers do—a critical lesson for young people to learn in this day and age.

Collecting rain at anchor

Slowing Down

Extended travel allows family members step out of the fast lane. It's a beautiful day that doesn't begin with chasing the children out of bed and off to school, then off to various practices and lessons—a beautiful day for parents and children alike. There's something truly special about observing and indulging each family member in his or her favorite pursuits. The minute hand of a clock takes on far less importance than the altitude of the sun, and appointments are usually kept on island time. Though sailing has its challenges, we've never felt such peace of heart on land. Living life at a pace you can dictate: it's not only healthy, it's magic.

Learning to Schedule Free Time

Extended travel gives children an opportunity to learn to schedule their own free time and to be creative. For some, this can be a challenge, but they'll soon come to appreciate the freedom and learn to make their own fun. Countless studies support the idea that "boredom" is beneficial to developing well-rounded young minds. Extended periods of cruising have shaped our son into a self-starter with a long attention span, because he can pursue his interests and complete projects without outside pressure.

Is There a Best Age?

If those are some of the benefits, what is the best age to take kids on an extended sailing adventure? That's a lot like trying to determine the best boat! There is no single right answer—only the answer that works best for you.

There are advantages and disadvantages to every age group. Some families set off with babies and we've heard them rave about how well it works, because a baby's needs are so few: loving parents, food, and sleep! Most families, however, chose to go cruising during their children's preschool or elementary school years. That's because young children are usually very flexible travelers and it's often considered easier to coach kids through elementary level learning experiences. Although children who accompany their parents on a Caribbean cruise at this age might not retain as many memories as their older siblings do, the experience will still impart them with a world view and intense family bond that will play a significant role in their formative years.

Other sailing families say that traveling with children between the ages of eight and twelve is best because these children are more mature and can study the world around them more deliberately. They can compare cultural differences, undertake more in-depth studies, and reflect on their experiences. They can be fairly independent and also follow directions—at least in theory! We have cruised with our son when he was four and again from the time he turned seven until he was ten. Both were rich, rewarding experiences in every way, and we couldn't possibly say which was better.

The vast majority of families who cruise for longer periods of time have children in these younger age groups. Fewer undertake a cruise with teens, but that doesn't mean it can't be done. These families are more likely to head out for strictly defined periods of time such as a semester or school year and often rely on packaged homeschooling programs to structure their academic work. The primary hurdles of sailing with teens are their greater need for social contact with their peer group and more specialized coursework. However, older kids are better able to make sense of what they experience and directly apply it in and outside of school. Most of the teen sailors we have met say the rewards far outweigh the sacrifices, and their parents agree. All in all, sailing with teens can be an incredibly rewarding (if trying) experience. In other words, it's not too different from raising a teen on land!

Sailing as a family – take the plunge!

Chapter 2

Activities for Underway

Sailing in the Caribbean can be a dream come true: a chance for families to slow down and gain priceless time together. But remember, Mom and Dad's (or Grandma and Grandpa's) idea of fun and a kid's idea of fun can be two vastly different things. For adults, sailing represents the chance to relax and escape the daily grind. Kids, on the other hand, equate relaxing with boredom. Ideally, we as sailing parents should be prepared with ideas that will not only keep the kids busy but also keep them tuned in to sailing and their surroundings.

Some of the pastimes listed below are active and exciting pursuits, while others are quieter and more contemplative. Most can be done on a basic level with very young children or adapted into a more involved challenge for older kids. None require a lot of preparation or materials: just get up and go!

Children As Active Crew

Sailing for hours from harbor to harbor quickly bores most kids unless they're involved in operating the boat: steering, trimming, raising the sail. But even this can grow monotonous for youngsters, and they'll soon seek stimulation elsewhere. A second problem is that the sheer size and forces

9

on most cruising boats make it difficult for younger kids to be involved safely. Our son couldn't even see over the dodger of our thirty-five foot sloop on our first Caribbean cruise! For him, steering meant constantly eying the compass. Not exactly a barrel of laughs, much as he liked the responsibility.

Luckily, there are many other ways to keep the kids involved in boat operations. Hourly log book entries are one, since even very young children can learn to make weather observations, read a barometer, check the GPS, and even plot a position on a chart. Yes, that's right—a good old-fashioned chart, one with a large enough scale to give a gratifying feeling of progress. While sailing, kids can measure the distance to the next anchorage, learn various GPS functions, and estimate true wind speed and direction—all of which reinforce broader skills they'll have picked up or will soon be addressing in school (measurement, estimation, land features, and so on). Referring to charts frequently will also help a child learn the geography of an area and thus develop a sense of what "the Caribbean" really means.

Another way to keep kids tuned in to sailing is to assign them the task of making a movie—not just filming various clips, but editing them into a movie that chronicles a specific aspect of the trip. They might focus on "a typical day aboard," capturing a bit of everything from breakfast and weighing anchor to sailing, lunch, and evening activities on board. Alternatively, your young cinematographer might choose to film an original story, spoof a television program, or make a sailing how-to. Anything goes!

To develop organizational skills at the same time, have the kids approach this assignment in multiple steps, from brainstorming what they should include and outlining their movie to actually moving on to production (a process similar to outlining an essay). Make the assignment as specific as possible, such as a three minute movie in which no single clip runs longer than fifteen seconds with different transitions between segments and a credit section at the end. If your kids aren't already familiar with self-editing software like Microsoft Movie Maker, they'll quickly learn because most of these programs are self-explanatory. Not only is moving-making a fun activity, it also creates a nice souvenir of your trip.

Monitor Resources

Another way of keeping kids tuned in is to assign them the job of monitoring your resources. How much water do the tanks hold? What is the battery capacity on board? What about fuel? A boat equipped with solar or wind power connected to a charge control unit has the makings of a thought-provoking lesson. Watch what happens when the sails shade the solar panels or when a burst of wind hits the wind generator. See (or even graph) how input varies as conditions change or at different times of day.

There's nothing like limiting a previously unlimited resource to teach a child the value of an amp! We bought our son his own small solar panel with which to charge his electronic devices. He learned to position the panel and to ration his power use so that his Kindle and MP3 player stayed charged. It's a valuable life lesson in renewable energy sources and energy consumption, available for under $50. A side benefit we parents appreciated was the natural cap this placed on the time he could spend on his devices. Once the power was out, he had to get out a book, build Lego, or just get creative with whatever he found on board.

Make and Tow a Toy

Very young children will enjoy designing and making things to tow behind the boat. Start by chopping a foot-long section off a foam swim noodle. Then carve and decorate it into, say, a sea dragon. Run a line through a hole in the noodle and you'll be ready to launch and tow your creation. On day two, you can use the next section of swim noodle to carve something else, like a sea serpent, and have the two monsters race. On day three, you can make a crocodile. On day four... well, you get the picture.

Alternatively, have the kids collect sticks, twigs, or popsicle sticks on land and later build a miniature raft to tow on the way to your next destination. The more complex the construction, the better. All of these creations have their own special style of movement and opportunities for

11

tweaking toward perfection. The latter is an important point: encourage your kids to improve each design rather than seeing things as one-time, one-try, disposable entertainment. After all, being on a boat is the perfect setting in which to encourage longer attention spans and a tinkerer's approach.

Enjoy designing and towing a toy

Data Collection

Another fun pastime is a two-step process that can later be taken to a higher level to hone mathematics skills. First, decide on a point of interest and make a tally of observations: for example, how many types of birds, boats, or seashells can you find? Instead of being bored, the kids will have an activity to keep them tuned into their surroundings with a specific task. Later, you can pull out colored pencils and paper to graph the results. A simple bar graph will do for younger kids while a composite bar graph is more challenging for older children. It doesn't have to be a work of mathematical perfection to reinforce skills learned in school.

Collecting, displaying, and analyzing data are also important aspects of scientific studies. Have kids summarize their findings in words. Do different anchorages show different "populations" of boats? Why does a certain kind of fish or coral predominate in an area you snorkel over? You can even repeat the study on a different occasion to see if repeat observations bring similar results, something every good scientist does.

Reading and Writing

A quiet activity all family members will enjoy is reading aloud to each other, either during a passage or an evening at anchor. In our modern era of multiple stimulations, it's nice to slow things down and have all ears concentrate on a single voice. Soon a hush will fall over everyone, allowing a family bonding experience that also inspires the imagination. Each member of the family can read a few pages, then pass along the book for the next reader. Our family has very strong memories of reading the *Adventures of Sherlock Holmes* on many a tropical night, our spines tingling from the creepy tales, as well as the times we laughed ourselves silly over a Cornelia Funke tale. In the end, it's all about being together and sharing.

Another fun activity is a writing exercise we call pass-it-on story time. Have the whole family sit down together, each person with a sheet of paper and pencil. After a minute of quiet thinking, everyone begins to

13

write a story—any story. After two minutes, each person passes their paper to the left and receives one from the right. Now each writer gets two minutes to continue the broken-off story they just received. *What will the mischievous boy do next? Where do the adventurous bats fly for their next adventure? Just how will our heroine bring those pirates to justice?* It's amazing how quickly stories can snowball and take wild, unexpected, and fun turns.

Continue until each person has contributed to each story. During the last round, writers must be sure to conclude the eclectic stories (allow a little extra time if needed). Then it's time to read the results aloud. Our sessions usually end in hearty laughs, with a good time had by all. This activity reinforces important writing skills such as recognizing the parts of a story, connecting ideas, and above all, creative writing. Very young children can participate by partnering with an older scribe. You can also turn this into a verbal exercise. Each person adds a few sentences to a single story that can take countless twists and turns as the wind steadily propels you toward your destination for the day.

Chapter 3

Activities at Anchor

Generally, it's easier to design fun activities for time at anchor because you have a more stable platform from which to work as well as the opportunity to explore away from the boat—or even around it. The possibilities are endless!

Adventure

There's nothing like an adventure to whet a young sailor's appetite for more. Swimming and snorkeling rank high on the list, and the key to keep things interesting is to turn them into a challenge. Can the kids dive deep and see what the keel looks like? How about checking the rudder? Can they dive all the way under the boat from port to starboard? From bow to stern? You can hold a cannonball or diving contest and strike different poses in the air, or bring out the water pistols and have a skirmish—anything to keep it fun.

Of course, there's always the chance to explore a nearby reef and its colorful inhabitants. Some kids, however, might find it pointless to paddle around just looking at things. *Looking at what?* they'll ask. The best counter-measure is to turn snorkeling into a treasure hunt. Bring along a waterproof fish identification guide and see how many species you can find. Better yet, assign the kids specific targets. Can they spot a butterfly fish? A blue tang? What about a needlefish? The trick is to make the quest challenging yet reasonable enough to keep success rates high. The more specific you are, the easier it will be for your child to focus. For example, how many of the fish in the second row of your fish chart can you find today? You can bring a waterproof camera along on the second or third snorkel expedition to keep the activity fresh. Alternatively, you could have the kids tally and compare results from different anchorages. Parents wishing to tie in to school lessons could easily turn this into the basis for a report or a graphing exercise.

You can do the same with beach combing by bringing along a good field guide to seashells. We carried a variety of field guides aboard our sloop, including the *Smithsonian Handbook to Shells* by Peter Dance and its partner volume, *Whales, Dolphins, and Porpoises* by Mark Carwardine, and used them to expand our horizons. Another favorite is star-gazing, and a good book like H.A. Rey's classic *The Stars* will not only help you find constellations, but understand the stories behind them, too. Our son spent many a fruitful hour over Pat Murphy's *The Klutz Guide to the Galaxy* which includes star maps, a red-bulbed reading light, and a kit to make a simple telescope.

Science and Mapping

Mapping an anchorage is another adventurous activity that will keep kids aware of their surroundings. This can be as simple or as complex as you like. We spent an enjoyable afternoon out in the dinghy with a lead line and handheld GPS, collecting data points with our eight-year-old and his friends. Afterwards, he used graph paper to create a map that also included the outline of a small "treasure island." Not only is the exercise fun, it also reinforces math and art skills. Related activities like geocaching and treasure hunts will keep the kids alert to their unique surroundings in a similar way.

A sailboat can be equal parts playground and physics lab. We've had kids spend an enjoyable hour hoisting stuffed animals aloft, climbing the mast (with a safety harness and belay), and lifting objects with increasingly complex block and tackle arrangements. Even if you don't go for an all-out science lesson, you'll see that the possibilities are limitless. Another hour of fun can easily be had in a sandcastle (or sand sculpture) session on the beach—an activity that typically draws in curious on-lookers and thus creates the opportunity to make new acquaintances.

Sailboat = playground + science lab

17

Photography

Taking field trips to various land sights is another great exercise. One way to put the spark into a field trip is to hand your kids a camera and make it into a photo safari. Parents who like to add an academic slant to things can assign a photo essay (rather than an actual report), which means downloading, selecting, and briefly annotating the best shots once you're back from the trip (see *Photo Essays*). This really helps kids seek out the details of a historic fortress or an area of great natural beauty. Older kids can start to learn about composing a balanced image and making the most of the camera's settings. A camera is also a good way to encourage interaction with local kids, who rarely tire of posing for shots and laughing over the results. That's the beauty of digital photography: instant gratification and the ability to click away at no cost. And who knows? You might just get an award-winning photo or two out of the results.

Writing

If you're looking for a quieter, more contemplative activity, devote time to journal writing, either while under way or in the evenings. Sailing in the Caribbean bombards the senses with hundreds of new impressions every day. In fact, that's one way to prompt a journal entry: focusing on senses other than sight. What were the smells, tastes, and textures of the day?

While we usually think of a journal as a single book in which to record memories, a journal can also be a collection of postcards that have been written on (whether they are actually sent or simply collected as keepsakes). This is an especially good way for young children to start a journal, because the field in which to write only calls for so much text and the picture creates a natural writing prompt. Very young children can dictate their impressions to a parent who acts as a scribe. Another way to keep journals interesting is to draw or paste in maps, souvenirs, or other elements of a collage. You can look for postage stamps that show a swath of scenery or a bird, then paste these into the journal and have the kids use their imaginations to draw a scene around it. This certainly livens up a humdrum "today we did... and then we....and after that we... " type of journal entry.

The next step up, of course, is creative writing. You might start with a prompt like "We were playing on the beach when around the corner came a pirate ship and..." Alternatively, use your children's favorite books as inspiration to weave a new yarn. My son enjoyed writing his own "Magic School Bus in the Caribbean" story, putting himself in the tale and making the bus transform into a boat. Oh, the adventures they had! In his *Little Dragon Coconut* phase, he circumnavigated the globe in a writing activity that extended over several months. To take things to the next level, your child can illustrate the story or create a comic strip of the main events.

Having listed all these activities, I'll take a step back now and move on to an equally important point: sometimes, it's best not to entertain the kids at all but let them find their own entertainment. Encouraging kids to do so develops creativity, a fact reinforced by many studies. It's amazing what a kid can do with a deck of cards, a bucket of water, or a blank sheet of paper. Allowing kids quiet time will also allow them to delve into their own interests instead of simply absorbing whatever is set in front of them like a ready-made meal. Let them become creators instead of consumers. At first, this can be hard work for the twenty-first-century kid who is accustomed to a constant barrage of media and electronic distractions. That, however, only makes the exercise all the more valuable. Take heart: home-made entertainment gets easier with every blue-sky day and every star-lit night.

Chapter 4

Keeping Cruising Kids Tuned in to the Caribbean

We take our children cruising to show them a new part of the world and to enjoy a wonderful lifestyle in step with nature. However, if you want your children to come away from the experience with new knowledge or a new perspective, you should conscientiously cultivate an approach that will tune them in to the Caribbean. Leave the DVDs and Game Boys at home (or at least in the bunk) because they tend to isolate children from their surroundings. Activities like the ones described in this chapter will encourage your kids to actively explore, observe, and critically examine details that might otherwise go unnoticed. School children often complain that their lessons aren't related to real life—but on a boat in the Caribbean, they'll enjoy intriguing, real-life learning at its best!

Product Origins

You can start over breakfast. Where did the milk come from? What about the cereal or the syrup? Just think about it for a moment. Those of us hailing from North America give little thought to such things: the cows are the countryside and the milk is trucked over to my town, right? But what about the Caribbean, with its scattered islands and proud but tiny nations? Surely little Canouan, for example, does not produce every item on the store shelves. So where do the supplies come from? What are the implications of off-island trade?

Challenge kids to read grocery labels to establish the origin of each item. I was surprised to find that milk in Antigua's large supermarkets is imported from Florida, for example. Yogurt in St. Vincent comes from Martinique, while Grenada seems to be the regional producer of baking flour. Trinidad, on the other hand, has the distinction of being the Caribbean's local producer of toilet paper. Sugar is another interesting item: while refined sugar is often available at exorbitant prices, natural brown sugar is much cheaper—exactly the opposite of the situation in a North American or European store.

There are several things you can do with this information. The first is to turn it into a geography lesson. Pull out a map and chart your breakfast, so to speak. This will illustrate the point well. Second, discuss the implications. Some cruisers complain about the high price of goods in the Caribbean, but there is a good reason for that. How do goods reach store shelves? Why does that make the price go up? How dependent are islanders on outside goods? What is locally produced? What are local specialties? Of course, you could focus an entire college course on this topic, but even children can begin to consider it. In doing so, they will be critical thinkers, questioning and researching the world around them instead of barely taking notice.

The next step is to take a field trip to an island supermarket. Better yet, two field trips: one to a large supermarket and one to a small corner shop. Come supplied with a list of items you usually stock and research where each comes from (bread, toothpaste, fruit, etc). Then compare results between the two stores: does the corner store offer more local products than the supermarket? Don't be shy: ask the small shop owner questions about where his or her products come from and how deliveries work.

This exercise accomplishes several things: it opens children's eyes to the realities of commerce on island communities and helps them appreciate why their favorite treats might not be on offer everywhere. Environmentally conscious sailors understand the importance of buying locally—another theme you can tie in to. What are the environmental costs of shipping milk to Antigua? What does a locally produced meal on Guadeloupe consist of? Maybe you can even make a project of cooking one up!

Currency

This leads to another interesting theme: money. In the Eastern Caribbean, you will come across the colorful EC dollar as well as the Euro on French islands. It can be fun to study coins and bills in detail. Currency can contain a lot of information, including important people (contemporary or historic), sights, or valued cultural icons and symbols. On EC bills, you will find many interesting images: Queen Elizabeth, Nobel Prize-winner Sir Arthur Lewis, Brimstone Hill Fortress, sea turtles, and nutmeg. This study can lead in several different directions. You can pull out the map and locate featured sites, for starters. Are any close enough to visit? Then research the people: Who was Sir Arthur Lewis? Why the Queen of England? How do the themes on the local currency compare with those from your home country? What does the choice of decoration reveal about cultural values?

Take a close look. What can you learn?

Currency also lends itself well to mathematical exercises for conversion rates. If EC$2.70 equals US$1, how many EC dollars makes US$10? How many US dollars is EC$100? You can also convert EC dollars to Euro, Euro to US dollars, and so on. Young children can work with coins and parts of one hundred. You can then turn to real life examples, such as postage and stamps, another promising topic. How much does it cost to send a postcard home from St. Vincent and how does this compare to postage rates in Martinique? If you had to do a mass mailing, which postal system would you use to save money? Children might also enjoy starting a mini stamp collection. Stamps can be used to decorate a journal or to create a postage-stamp map of the Caribbean, island by island, country by country.

Another interesting activity is a comparative treasure hunt of mailboxes. Yes, mail boxes. While modern, utilitarian mailboxes abound, you can also find a number of special models. The Commonwealth countries usually have red boxes with *ER* imprinted on them (*Elizabeth Regina* or Queen Elizabeth), and a few even have vintage *GR* boxes (*George Rex*) from the time of her father, King George VI. In this way, clues to local history can be revealed. Kids can make a rubbing or take a picture of such "collector's items."

Enjoying Nature

On a completely different note, make sure to expose your children to the spectacular natural beauty of the Caribbean. Don't limit yourself to the coast and beaches: visit a rainforest, botanical garden, or one of the many stunning waterfalls in the islands. Bring a notebook and camera to record what you see and assign specific "targets" for each child to observe and describe. What types of bird can you see? How big are the lizards? Are they camouflaged? What was the animal doing (foraging, resting, moving)? How exactly do vines cling? What patterns can you find within a flower? Making specific observations helps children focus and remember rich details they would otherwise have missed if simply looking at the general view.

One good place for an excursion into a nature preserve is the Indian River in Dominica, where a trained guide can point out hard-to-spot animals and interesting vegetation and answer questions along the way. Make sure you tell your guide what you are after so that his keen eyes and local knowledge will complement your children's research. The Indian River is a wonderful destination because it feels adventurous and even young children can participate (more on this in *Part III: Field Trips*).

Let's face it: long hikes are rarely inspiring for children. However, you can turn a hike into an adventure by having a clear goal: reaching a "secret" waterfall or mysterious rock carvings. The same idea can be applied to the underwater world. Don't just jump in and look randomly; snorkel with a specific purpose. For example, study the movement of stingrays along a sandy bottom. Which way do their "wings" move when they swim and when they settle on the bottom? If you spot a turtle, study its movements from a distance. Where is it looking for food? What is it eating? Doing so may not turn your child into the next Jacques Cousteau, but it will cement the experience more firmly into his or her young mind.

Art

At some point, take the time for an art project. Just sit your child down in front of a lovely view (take your pick— there's no shortage!) or concentrate on one small object, like a shell or a flower, and let him or her draw. The idea is not to create a masterpiece but rather to take the time to carefully observe shapes, contours, and the interplay of color. Kids can use crayons, pencils, watercolors—anything. Their perspective might be way off, or the outcome more abstract than intended, but the important thing is the process, not the product. Parents should be good role models and make their own artwork. For a different art form, carve a block of soap into the shape of an animal or seashell. Soap is soft and easy to work with so there's no need for sharp tools. The peace and reflection that art carries with it will bring kids a little step closer to their subject matter. Ideally, you'll also end up with a special keepsake or a homemade gift for a friend.

Making New Friends

Finally, help your children get out and talk to local people. Share beach toys with local children and start up a friendly exchange. We had many fascinating and eye-opening conversations with friendly people throughout the Caribbean. Traveling with a child opens doors. Many local people are more than happy to talk about life in their corner of the Caribbean with a curious, friendly, and genuinely interested visitor. Older children interested in a particular topic can even set up an interview. All you have to do is ask! Start with "I am doing a project on groceries in the Caribbean. May I ask you a few questions?" You will find people pleased to be asked and more than willing to devote their attention to your inquiries.

Vendors can be excellent conversationalists as long as you find them at a quiet moment. A talkative vendor, if you find one, can be a goldmine of information. We often found women who were justifiably proud of their small but successful enterprises and full of mesmerizing stories. Children can ask about sports, hobbies, or school life on their host island. They are likely to uncover a number of differences to their home systems, but also many similarities.

Children can start by eavesdropping on their parents' conversations, or prepare a few questions and start with someone in the tourism industry. Service providers such as "boat boys" are often happy to relate their personal stories: how they got started, how they worked their way up from surfboard to outboard, what they do in the off-season, etc. Older people will proudly relate their memories of the day their home island went from colony to independence, another promising topic for discussion. Whatever you do, don't isolate your children from the local population, especially when a unique opportunity presents itself.

To preserve all these experiences, have your child keep a journal. Just a few sentences written on a regular basis will do. This helps children review and reflect on the day. Without a journal, your child will collect a string of pleasant but vague memories. With a journal, the chances of putting together pieces of an interlocking puzzle with sharper focus increase. Your children will come away with new knowledge, new questions, and new perspectives on their lives back home. You might even encourage your children to see themselves as travel writers reporting on the Caribbean. They can produce *A Kid's Guide to St. Lucia*, or write a fictional story set in the Caribbean, filling the background with details they have observed and characters they have met.

These suggestions are all mini adventures, not chores. Get out and get close; open yourself to the unfamiliar and the unexpected. Any of these activities could be the subject of a more extensive study, too. Just adapt these ideas to your child's developmental level and your family's commitment to on-board education, whether that's casual or more formal. Leading your children through inquiries like those described here can also foster a sense of family accomplishment that lingers long after your time in the tropics comes to a bittersweet end.

Making new friends

Part II

LOCATIONS

There are hundreds of wonderful places throughout the Caribbean and dozens of travel and cruising guides to help you find them. I'll leave the exhaustive coverage to those books and concentrate on a get-started guide to our favorite Caribbean haunts. The first chapter in this section draws on our family's own sailing experiences and whittles down a long list of favorites to the top ten in the Windward and Leeward Islands, plus a few honorable mentions and places farther afield.

The second chapter covers the top ten family-friendly places and activities in the British Virgin Islands, thanks to contributing author, Captain Bob Daigle. I can't imagine a better source of information than Bob and his wife Maggie, who have cruised the BVIs for years, specializing in family charters.

Of course, ten families asked to complete this exercise would produce ten different lists! Often, all it takes is for just the right (or wrong) person to walk along the beach to change your impression of a place. And sometimes, the most memorable places are the unexpected gems that you discover on your own. In that spirit, we look forward to hearing from families who'd like to nominate their own "top ten" lists!

Great places in the Caribbean: take your pick!

Chapter 5

Top Ten Spots for Kids in the Eastern Caribbean (and Beyond)

In this chapter, we the crew of *Namani* have put our heads together to produce a list of favorite family-friendly spots in the Eastern Caribbean. How did we judge our top ten? The primary criteria was simply how memorable each place was. Sometimes, that came from the sheer natural beauty of the location. In other cases, it was thanks to convenience, a unique point of interest, or the overall feel of a place. We hope you enjoy these spots and are soon able to add ten of your own to the list!

Les Saintes, Guadeloupe

If there was only one spot we could visit in all the Caribbean, this little archipelago would be it. Lying ten miles south of Guadeloupe, these islands define "tranquility." On the main island, Terre-de-Haut, things only pick up when the ferry comes in; after that, sleepy dogs drop right back into their naps in the middle of the street. The beaches are gorgeous and there are several to choose from (both protected and more exposed). Our

The stunning beach at Les Pitons

favorite was Grande Anse, the long sandy strip on the windward side. Although it is too rough for swimming, it's perfect for sandcastle-building and general cavorting in the sand. Terre-de-Haut is a wonderful place for long walks, baguette or croissant in hand. Historic forts stand atop both crests of the main bay, including colonial-era Fort Napoleon where the kids can explore moats, cannons, and the echoing halls of the interior.

Quiet as Terre-de-Haut is, its bucolic little sister, Terre-de-Bas, is even quieter, being an island off an island off an island. Though there are no major sights to visit, we loved the friendly, laid-back vibe of the place. Over on Terre-de-Haut, you'll hear the mosquito-like noise of mopeds regularly (though we never found them to be a nuisance), but in Terre-de-Bas, three vehicles an hour counts as traffic, and we enjoyed long exploratory walks. When our young son fell and scraped his knee, a woman promptly came out of her house with a bag of ice for him, forever cementing our love for this place.

Tobago Cays

The Tobago Cays are a must on any cruiser's itinerary and an aquatic wonderland for kids. There are several small islands to explore, whether that means climbing to their modest heights for a view or playing on the small strips of sand. Because the islands are protected national park territory, there's no development, giving the place a Robinson Crusoe feel. Even with dozens of boats anchored there, you'll have the feeling of being anchored on the edge of the world, since you can anchor in the lee of the reef and look out into an endless ocean view. The chances of seeing sea turtles are high. They can be spotted feeding in the shallows or swimming throughout the anchorage. For a bigger adventure, we hired a local fisherman to take us beyond the reef to tiny Petit Tabac, where the castaway scene in *Pirates of the Caribbean* was filmed.

Dominica

Dominica is one of the greenest, wildest islands in the Eastern Caribbean: a nature-lover's paradise. For families anchored in commodious Prince Rupert Bay, the first stop is often a boat tour up the Indian River. You're required to take a local guide with a hand-oared boat. We usually prefer to take excursions on our own but this is a good way to support the local economy. Our guide did a wonderful job explaining various plants to the children and delighting them with little birds he fashioned out of leaves. Trees and vines overhang the river, so it's a small, safe adventure that will fascinate young and old.

Other attractions require a rental car or a van and driver, but are extremely worthwhile (and relatively inexpensive if shared between several crews). Our visit to Kalinago Barana Autê, a cultural center on the windward side of the island, remains one of the top highlights of our Caribbean cruise. There, you will meet descendants of indigenous Caribs who mixed with escaped slaves and found safe haven on this wild side of the island during colonial times. Your family will have a personal guide to show you around a recreated village and explain the culture and history of the Kalinago.

As the last surviving community with indigenous roots anywhere in the Eastern Caribbean, it's a fascinating place. A trip here segues neatly into discussions the impact that Columbus and subsequent colonial powers had on local populations.

Elsewhere on Dominica, you can hike to waterfalls, search for the colorful Sisserou parrot that graces the national flag, and swim in jungle pools. It's impossible to overlook the poverty on this island, but just as striking is the natural beauty and the pride and resourcefulness of its people.

Bequia

Ah, Bequia. There's just something about the laid-back vibe of this island that makes every sailor smile. For families, the attractions are many, starting with a huge, safe harbor where you're likely to find other sailing kids, plus a convenient main town. A walk to the windward side of the island will give the kids a fitness challenge on the way to some of the nicest beaches in the Caribbean. Once there, you can stake out your own spot among the palms and spend a happy afternoon doing as much or as little as you like. One point of interest on Bequia is the Old Hegg Turtle Sanctuary where young and old can observe hatching sea turtles up close and learn about conservation efforts (see the *Field Trips* section in Part III of this book for tips on how to turn an interesting outing into a rich educational experience).

Shirley Heights, Antigua

One of the most memorable evenings of our Caribbean cruise was the Sunday barbecue at Shirley Heights. Our kids were so fascinated by the steel drum band that they ended up dancing the night away with creative moves all their own. Young and not-so-young alike enjoyed the music, great food, and views, not to mention the atmospheric surroundings in an eighteenth-century fort. Throw in sunset over the Caribbean and you know why so many sailors (and landlubbers) rate the event so highly. The anchorage below in English Harbour gets cramped at peak times, but gives you a prime base for hiking to the Heights as well as exploring historic Nelson's Dockyard. If you're based in Jolly Harbour, consider renting a car to combine a day of errands with an evening of fun for all ages.

Grenada

Prickly Bay is one of those sheltered anchorages that boats come to visit for a week and end up spending a season. There's easy shore access to a small marina (with lots of space to anchor in the bay), a Budget Marine, and grassy areas where kids can unwind. When you're ready for a day out, rent a car or hire a driver to take you to the island's top sights: the working cocoa plantation on historic Belmont estate, the scenic yet sobering point at Carib's Leap near Sauteurs at the northern tip of the island, and Grand Etang National Park, where even young children can manage the trail to Seven Sisters Falls. Another island highlight for us was Fish Night in the town of Gouyave, where it seems half the town sets up food stalls in the streets while the other half eats. Excursions like these expose children to different environments and ways of life while fostering a sense of exploration and discovery. All in all, we found Grenada to be a very manageable, friendly island for family exploration or quiet days at anchor.

Les Pitons and Sulphur Springs, St. Lucia

Anse des Pitons isn't just one of the most scenic spots in the entire Caribbean; it's also a great spot for families in several ways. There's the stunning beach, for one, plus nearby Soufrière Sulphur Springs and Diamond Botantical Gardens for exploration farther inshore. Kids will be fascinated by the boiling sulphur springs and will enjoy time spent soaking in the nearby mineral baths. You'll have to pay for a mooring, but it's well worth it, considering the deep, rocky anchorage. Every morning begins with a new adventure and every evening with an incredible sunset. Elsewhere in St Lucia, we weren't impressed with the overdevelopment in Rodney Bay and Marigot Bay. Even though "progress" has crept into the Pitons area, nothing can dampen the sheer natural beauty of the place.

Barbuda

Antigua's partner island is a paradise of white sand beaches like the ten-kilometer long haven of Low Bay on the west side. Barbuda is not so much a place for inland exploration as for days of fun and sun in the sand. Here, you'll be able to stake out your own spot along the long coastline without the crowded feeling of other Caribbean anchorages. There's almost no development and not much to do but look for seashells and count the stars. Heaven, indeed!

Saint-Pierre, Martinique

You know you're in for something different when a harbor chart looks like a tic-tac-toe board full of Xs. These mark the graves of the ghosts of Saint-Pierre. The harbor, not much more than a slim indentation on Martinique's leeward coast, was packed with wooden schooners in March 1902. When neighboring Mount Pelée erupted in a pyroclastic burst, it instantly leveled the town and ignited the fleet. Today's cruisers must pick their spots with care: we got the point when a nearby boat struggled to free its fouled anchor from underwater wreckage. Even ghosts need amusement, it seems!

Today's Saint Pierre is a quiet and interesting, if eerie, place to visit. Reminders of the tragedy are everywhere, from the ashy beach to blackened ruins still dotting the town. A museum chronicles the town's early days and the fiery end of an era, and visitors can also visit the stone jail cell where a convict weathered the catastrophe as the town's lone survivor.

Despite its sad past, Saint Pierre is full of cheerful, friendly faces. Almost inexplicably, we were drawn back here again and again. Our son and his buddies enjoyed the black sand beach and were fascinated by walks around town while we adults enjoyed the tree-lined, oh-so-French boulevard and unassuming character of the place. There are waterfront cafés and a convenient market with fresh fruit. And the ghosts, for their part, keep a low profile. Just don't tempt them with your anchor!

Visiting Brimstone Hill Fortress

Saint Kitts

Another island with multiple attractions for families is Saint Kitts. We spent a happy week sitting out high winds in White House Bay in the south, where we saw more Vervet monkeys than people. It's a scrubby, wild area that's perfect for family down time. When the wind dropped, we visited Basseterre with its quaint colonial center and made a trip out to Brimstone Hill Fortress, a UNESCO World Heritage site. The well-preserved fortress is touted as "a monument to the ingenuity of the British military engineers who designed it and to the skill, strength and endurance of the African slaves who built and maintained it." Whichever side of the equation you emphasize to your children, it's a great place to climb on cannons, play soldier, and study history.

Honorable Mentions

The above are our personal favorites, but the list could easily have been stretched to fifteen or twenty. Our first honorable mention goes to the island of Marie-Galante (off Guadeloupe) for its gorgeous beaches, quiet lanes, and historic plantations. We're usually don't to go for packaged entertainment, but a day in the small water park at Anse d'Arlet on Martinique was just the ticket for our son, who could have spent days enjoying the floating trampolines and climbing structures there. For life in the slow lane, long walks ashore on the islands of Carricacou, Mayreau, and Anguilla scored high on our list. Farther north and west, one of our favorite spots is Culebra in the Spanish Virgin Islands—a quiet haven so delightfully unlike the heavily trafficked waters of the British and U.S. Virgin Islands to the east.

Elsewhere in the Caribbean

The Eastern Caribbean is just one logical cruising ground, but the entire sea basin is full of gems, some of them hidden, others well-known. Panama's San Blas islands top many a "favorites" list and make an excellent family destination. There's snorkeling, safe swimming, and interactions with the fascinating Kuna population. We spent a week anchored off an islet in the East Lemmon Cays where kids from four boats spent every waking hour playing together on shore. The handful of Kuna inhabiting the fishing camp on the island were gracious hosts who invited our children into their thatched buildings to observe them making meals or sewing molas (the appliqué needlework the islands are known for).

Portobelo, not far west along the same coast, showed us the grittier side of Panama (the pollution and structural decay are impossible to overlook), but we came to love the town nonetheless. Kids can explore the Spanish fortresses ringing the bay for fun or as part of an educational field trip. Adults will enjoy getting to know members of the international cruising community anchored there.

For all the warnings we were given not to visit Jamaica, we loved every minute of our week-long stay in Port Antonio. The anchorage is secure, the town convenient, and the locals friendly. Everyone took pains to make us feel at home, from customs officials to the staff of Errol Flynn Marina, street vendors, and just your average passers-by. The town is the gateway to the Blue Mountains, a rugged expanse carpeted with lush jungle and dotted with red flowers aptly named Flame of the Forest. Rafting down the Rio Grande makes for a memorable day trip that supports local enterprises in an environmentally friendly way. We spent a day with the amiable Captain Debbo, who not only taught our son to pole his thirty-foot bamboo raft but even indulged us with an hour-long swim call in the deliciously cool, fresh water.

Chapter 6

Family Fun in the British Virgin Islands

Many thanks to Captain Bob Daigle for contributing this chapter!

A family sailing adventure in the British Virgin Islands presents a wonderful opportunity for an outdoor, family-centric, turn-off-the-electronics bonding experience. For the past several years, my wife Maggie and I have run a crewed charter catamaran in the British Virgin Islands, specializing in families with children as our guests. We hope you enjoy your time in the BVIs and that our ideas and suggestions help your family make the most of these incredible cruising grounds. Some of our favorite BVI spots and activities for families with kids are listed below. They are all worthwhile and are listed in no particular order.

Fish Light at Night

Almost every single mooring or anchorage in the BVIs teems with tarpon, muscular three-foot-long fish. Despite their size, these fish are completely safe since they have no teeth and cannot bite. They are shy during the daytime, so you may not see any while snorkeling—but put out a fish light at night and they come running! Watching these fish as they swim off the stern of the boat is entertaining in itself. Although they appear rather slow and lazy, these fish are in the top five fastest in the ocean and occasionally you'll see evidence of this behind your boat. Interestingly, tarpon prosper principally because they don't taste good and thus aren't harvested for commercial purposes.

Have a bold teen? Let him or her quietly enter the water and swim with a school of thirty tarpon. Teens also love surreptitiously slipping over the bow and quietly swimming between the hulls of a catamaran to surprise the crew at the stern when they set off a splash-filled commotion among the fish gathered there. This will scare the fish away, but also provides a funny shocker for all who have been quietly watching. Otherwise, just lay on your belly with your head over the stern rail and enjoy the show.

We suggest going online and buying a fish light to bring to the Caribbean with you. I have boarded airplanes carrying my fish light inside my carry-on baggage. They aren't too expensive, are usually low consuming LEDs, and can generally plug into the 12V or inverted 120V outlets on board.

White Bay, Jost van Dyke

Arrive at White Bay early and grab a mooring for the night. The beaches are great and host several famous beach bars, a volleyball net on the easternmost slice of beach, and a shallow harbor with pristine water and a white sandy bottom. This is one of the rare spots where you can see tarpon swimming in shallow water in daytime. A nighttime fish light will sometimes draw thirty or more tarpon.

We recommend late afternoon snorkeling in the crook in the far corner of the easternmost beach. Every so often, tarpon chase bait fish into the area, and you will be swimming inches away. White Bay is also good for paddle boarding but be careful when swimming off the boat since there are always dinghies zooming back and forth. It is best to take a dinghy or paddleboard when venturing into the beach rather than swimming the distance.

Muskmelon Bay, Guana Island

Muskmelon Bay is our favorite harbor in the BVIs. There are approximately fifteen moorings there, though the harbor is seldom visited. In part, this is due to exposure to the northerly swell, so visiting crews should be cautious. You can check in with dive shops anywhere in the BVIs for swell conditions. They are a great source of information and are always tuned into the sea state.

Most days, this harbor is terrific. On the far north corner of Muskmelon Bay are some beautiful rock formations, all interestingly "bird-like" (the island itself looks like Big Bird to me). In this north corner is a concrete platform that leads to a surprisingly well-maintained path to the top of a promontory. The platform can make for a tricky landing but once you're there, a short hike up leads to stunning views with a vertigo-inducing drop at your feet. Be especially careful at this cliff-top location with young children!

The harbor is wide open and great for swimming and snorkeling along the entire shoreline, as well as island exploring by dinghy. This is our favorite spot for pulling a tube behind the dinghy and whipping the kids along in a spot reminiscent of Jurassic Park. In semi-swell conditions there is a terrific blow hole along the north side of the bay. As a bonus, there's a nearly unobstructed westerly view for sunsets—a rarity in the BVIs due to the island chain's east-west orientation.

Monkey Point, Guana Island

Don't miss snorkeling at Monkey Point on Guana Island. We have swum in schools of bait fish so thick you literally cannot see your outstretched fingers. Then a tarpon swims out of the mass, just inches away. Monkey Point and White Bay are the only two spots in all of the BVI where we have seen tarpon consistently in the daytime. Large schools of bait fish are an everyday occurrence here which is also unique throughout all the BVI. You might even be lucky enough to meet Sam, the giant grouper who can sometimes be found loitering under the moored boats.

Snorkeling – fun for all ages!

Tubing

Bring along an inflatable tube to tow behind your dinghy for hours of fun with the kids. Ideally, you'll have a powerful dinghy to whip the excited passengers around and around. This activity is guaranteed to tire out young riders and is also a great photo and video opportunity. We recommend a tube with a solid middle section, which seems safer than those with a doughnut hole in middle. Tubes can be bought for short money on the Internet and come packed in small boxes for transport. They provide a high octane activity for older, more adventurous kids. Another fun experience is a slooowwww ride with Mom and young kids being towed behind with junior "helping" the captain operate the dinghy.

Note: for everyone's safety, it is vital to have experience in towing people behind a speeding boat before you try this activity. Make sure all tube riders have snug life jackets secured and on. If you're new to this experience, get some advice and coaching from friendly yachties: just ask around.

Family Games

There is something absolutely beautiful about a family sitting at a table together and playing games that cause giggles, excitement, feigned anger, thinking faces, sheepish Dad expressions, and comic face contortions. Have each member of the family do some research prior to your trip and come prepared with a whole suite of games: some new, some familiar. Kids love teaching their parents how to play a new game.

Of all the games we've played, *Twisted Farkel* always seems to draw the most uproarious laughter. Charades under the stars is a perennial favorite and the bow of a boat makes a perfect stage. Story games also get everyone captivated. I will never forget the "Wolf Game" with our Austrian guests or the crazy insights gained from Maggie's "Forest Game." These games and many more can easily be found with a bit of Internet research.

Michael Bean's Pirate Show at Leverick Bay, Virgin Gorda

This show is held at Leverick Bay Resort at 5 p.m. almost every weeknight and is free and open to all (check with Leverick Bay Resort & Marina to confirm the schedule). Michael Bean, the pirate, has an act honed by years of strumming, singing, and saying as many words as possible that include "arrrrrr." What's the most popular letter in the pirate alphabet? You guessed it—arrrrr!

The show is roughly an hour long and is filled with pirate sing-along songs, quizzes, and group percussion with supplied "shakearrrrrs." My personal favorite is the conch-blowing contest where any and all give the conch blow a try. Kids are the best and particularly enjoy the ever-present "conch farts" that come from blowing incorrectly. Tip: buy a blowable conch from Tito and Leroy at the Leverick fuel dock and practice prior to the show. A conch also makes a great keepsake to take home. The Michael Bean Pirate Show is family-friendly and good fun. Feel free to wear pirate hats, patches, etc. to get into the mood. You won't be alone in your silly costumes!

Another Leverick Bay family favorite is the weekly Jumbie Show, where a local dance troupe puts on their act while balanced ten feet in the air on giant stilts. Inevitably, a conga line forms with everyone dancing between the stilts. Again, check online or call Leverick Bay Resort & Marina for scheduling details. And as a final note, the English-style phone booth on the Leverick dock is actually a working shower, free for all to use. Kids love this fun change of scene from the cramped boat shower!

Tracking the Adventure

Sailing in the BVIs is inevitably a big circle (perhaps marked with a series of zigs and zags for tacks, if you are so inclined). Even though the route is somewhat predictable, it is always interesting to chart your route. As a side note, actually sailing (and not motoring) while going east and upwind is a distressingly rare habit among BVI sailors. For my money, successfully tacking a boat and sailing to your destination can be amazingly good fun for the whole family. And remember: the definition of a sailboat race is whenever two sailboats see one another.

Before you begin your trip, buy a good-sized, laminated chart of the BVIs and some thin tape in different colors. Each night, elect someone to trace your route by marking it with the tape. Use creative symbols to record your activities. Make this a nightly ritual after dinner. Kids just love being in charge of this, and we were always fastidious with our location accuracy which helped everyone recall and relive the details of their adventure. It is amazing how quickly the days become a blur unless you use something like this to anchor recollections to.

Once updated, we put the chart up on the sliding door or bulkhead for all to see. This also sets the stage for a "what's up tomorrow" team planning meeting in which you can discuss the geography, weather, and wind patterns of the Virgin Islands. Pirate stories are an easy segue as you point out the various harbors along the coastlines. At the conclusion of a trip, the chart becomes an important keepsake and can be photographed to preserve the details of the route and adventure.

Tarpon Feeding at Saba Rock, Virgin Gorda

Each evening at 5 p.m. a small crowd of people gather along the dockside at Saba Rock for a fish feed—an occasion for the fish to do the eating. Kids can grab a piece of bait and engage in a serious tug-of-war with a five-foot long tarpon. Be ready to grab the youngest one's ankles to keep him or her dockside because these fish are strong! There is usually a big barracuda skulking around, but he is shy and keeps back. You can also see a large ancient anchor hidden right under the Saba ferry just a few feet away from the tarpon feed. Behind you, the salt water tank will be loaded with local lobsters, conch, various fish, and an especially ugly moray eel. Interesting for all, this tank is especially mesmerizing for the youngest kids in the family.

The museum alongside the restaurant is a good stop for pirate booty, and in past seasons there were two large toucans behind the restaurant. In the shop you will find a silver ingot that Mom, Dad or a strong teenager can heft (about fifty pounds).

Our Snorkeling Favorites

These are some of our most closely held secret spots to snorkel, so enjoy and don't spread the word too far!

- Diamond Cove, Jost van Dyke: Guaranteed turtles and access to the Bubbly Pool. Be careful not to swim in Bubbly Pool during northerly swell conditions.

- Muskmelon Bay and Monkey Point, Guana Island.

- The back side of Eustacia Island: An amazing and pristine reef just off the easternmost beach with more conch than anywhere else.

- The Dog Islands: There are several moorings around each of these islands, all with great snorkeling.

- The north side of Great Dog Island: Anchor carefully (no moorings) and swim to the beach. The reefs here are fading a bit, but still amazing.

- The Indians: A late afternoon arrival is the best to avoid crowds (you can always find a mooring for the night just around the corner at Norman Island). Circumnavigate the islands that form the Indians, but don't miss the reef just off the eastern side. This is seldom snorkeled, but the best part of the Indians in our opinion.

- Great Harbor, Peter Island: The whole coastline, especially the middle part, has surprisingly good snorkeling.

- Mountain Point, Virgin Gorda (see below).

- The Baths: It is important to arrive at The Baths mooring field as early as possible (8 a.m. or earlier) and do the land tour through the giant boulders before the crowds arrive. If you are moored at Leverick Bay, consider an early morning cab ride up and over the mountain to the Baths. You can then include a visit to Hog Heaven, a restaurant specializing in pork dishes located far up the mountain.

At The Baths, you first scramble through the boulders, then jump in the water. This snorkeling is unique in all the world. The jumble of boulders between the two beaches is a great spot to explore, as is the entire Baths coastline. We explore the many routes around and under the rocks. You should always be careful of dinghy traffic here. If you stay close to shore amongst the boulders, though, you will be fine.

There are countless other snorkeling locations throughout the BVIs. If the coast looks good, the snorkeling is good. Get creative in your snorkeling spots and you won't be disappointed. We suggest getting everyone outfitted with snorkel gear at home, making sure the mask, snorkel and flippers work and fit properly. A jaunt or two to the local pool for some practice and gear check-out is a smart and fun "pre-trip" investment.

Discover a new world

Snorkeling at Mountain Point, Virgin Gorda

This is some of the best snorkeling in the BVIs with a few daytime moorings available. The biggest draw is the dive-in pool located along the coastline about fifty meters south from the "point" of Mountain Point. You need to carefully explore the nooks and crannies along the coastline to find it, but if the seas are relatively calm, the whole family can dive under the ledge and pop up into a small pool. It is a bit intimidating but really a relatively easy and confidence-building snorkeling adventure. The more adventurous can climb the walls of this pool and jump in. Be careful, however: the water is deep in the middle but there is plenty of sharp coral and rock around the edges.

Many thanks to Captains Bob and Maggie Daigle for sharing their wealth of experience in this chapter!

Part III

EDUCATIONAL ACTIVITIES

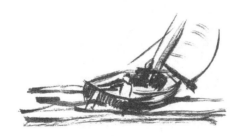

This section of the book addresses two of the biggest concerns of sailing parents: education and healthy development of social skills during an extended cruise. This is where you'll learn to design educational activities that enhance the take-away value of your child's experiences. You can tailor any of these suggestions to your own needs, whether that means casual learning experiences or structured homeschooling lessons. As a bonus, I've also included an extended excerpt from my book, *Lesson Plans Ahoy*. *The Voyages of Christopher Columbus* is an entire unit about the explorer and the impact of his discoveries on both sides of the Atlantic.

Nothing beats experience as education

Chapter 7

Six Tips for Home Schooling Sailors

Taking your children's education to sea is not always simple, but neither is it a complicated mystery. With careful decision-making and sensible preparations (just what you need for going cruising in general) you can let your children profit from an incredible learning opportunity. Yes, it does add an extra task to the cycle of watches, meal preparation, and boat maintenance, but homeschooling in such a unique situation can be rewarding for parents and children alike. You don't have to be setting off on a circumnavigation to think about educating afloat. A single season or even a week-long charter has endless possibilities, too.

Keep It Connected

Opportunities for authentic, hands-on learning experiences abound when you're cruising. Your children can snorkel on a reef or study dolphins. Visit a history museum, then sail in the wake of explorers and settlers. Even if you choose to follow a packaged homeschooling program, make sure your children are connected to the world around them. What phase is the moon in? When is the next high tide? What causes these phenomena?

A child's natural curiosity can be kindled with only a small hint, and you'll be off on an interesting lesson.

If your line lands a fish, take the time for a biology session before cooking it up. Later, link the experience to a lesson in animal adaptations or human physiology. This might be a more traditional lesson, but a child will be much more engaged now that he or she has had the fish dissection as a lead-in. These are just a few examples. You will quickly learn to identify and make the most of teachable moments. It does, however, require some finesse to shape a general interest lesson into one that also develops critical skills (more on this below).

Choose Carefully

Families setting sail for longer periods of time will need to carefully consider homeschooling choices (a topic covered in more detail in the book *Lesson Plans Ahoy*). Homeschooling packages such as those offered by the Calvert School are one convenient option. The advantages of these are the learning-by-numbers security they offer parents. All the planning is done, all the materials provided, and some degree of professional support is often included. Just by going to sea, however, you are taking yourself out of a cookie-cutter mold, so consider whether you want to use cookie-cutter learning for your kids. Packaged programs often include irrelevant or impractical lessons, such as complicated science experiments unsuited to a rocking platform or topics like the Industrial Revolution. Try getting your kids excited about that in, say, the Bahamas!

Other families create their own curriculum to suit their realities. Colonization and slavery are chapters of history that can be covered well in the Caribbean, and physics lessons can be found all over the boat. Learning can be completely student-centered, but you will be on your own in terms of materials, a problem that can be overcome with thorough research.

The greatest pitfall of independent curriculum design is the danger of leaving out difficult or inconvenient topics that are critical to developing literacy and numeracy skills. Even well-meaning, loving parents might subtly transfer their own passions to their children while sweeping their weaknesses under the carpet. You can avoid this trap by following standards from your school district at home and referring to them periodically. Ask yourself: have we covered the depth and breadth of this curriculum? Did we practice all the required math and science skills?

Families with two or more children should consider what their choice of program means in practical terms. If you use packaged programs, your children will be following unrelated strands of work which creates quite the juggling act. With a more independent approach, you can use a one-room schoolhouse approach in which everyone tackles the same topics but at different levels. While the youngest tracks his or her own water consumption and learns to make simple pictographs, the oldest can track overall water consumption on board and learn about graphic displays such as line graphs or pie charts. You will still be managing a circus, but at least all the action is in one ring! (See the *Age-Appropriate Adaptations* section of *The Voyages of Christopher Columbus* for examples of how to tailor work to various age groups.)

A number of useful resources exist for families who take homeschooling to sea. I have compiled many on a website, *www.sailkidsed.net*, including links to curriculum documents and a list of useful books and educational websites.

Do Your Homework

Most school districts provide full curricular documents online, making it possible to download a list of standards, benchmarks and/or learning outcomes for every subject area and grade (these detail what your child should be able to do at the end of each unit in each grade level). I am a firm believer that parents who homeschool their children must conscientiously use such standards to guide their work. This requires some finesse, as the following examples demonstrate, but you will develop a knack for it.

Let's say the kids are excited about volcanoes, for instance. In many prime sailing destinations, you will be among active, inactive, or extinct volcanoes, so conducting a basic lesson on volcanoes and geology will be easy. Now check your list of standards for literacy and mathematics. How can you pull those in? Take Virginia's grade two literacy standards, which include: "The student will write stories, letters, and simple explanations." That means step two is writing an explanation of how volcanoes work, including self-editing and details like: "Use correct spelling for high-frequency sight words, including compound words and regular plurals." Now check the math standards, where you will find: "The student, given grid paper, will estimate and then count the number of square units needed to cover a given surface in order to determine area." Adapt this by using a map and estimating the area your local volcano occupies. In this way, you encourage your child's interests and keep learning real while developing subject-specific skills.

To help judge how your travel plans will impact your child's schooling, schedule an appointment with your child's school to discuss your trip. If you're thinking about a cruise of a few weeks or months after which your child will return to the same classroom, talk to his or her teacher about the subjects that will be covered in your absence. Ideally, you'll find parallel learning opportunities. For example, if the school's upcoming science unit covers ecosystems, you can substitute an ecosystem in your destination while meeting the same unit criteria. Does the curriculum call for story writing? Use your travels as inspiration. Your children can stay connected to classmates through a weekly blog.

I recommend printing out complete curriculum documents and stocking up on books and materials before setting off. You might be able to purchase textbooks used by your school district and use them either in a traditional approach or within your own tailor-made program. The difficulty is in knowing what is useful and what is not before you actually set sail. Sorry, there is no easy answer here!

Keep It Fun

Learning can be fun! If you find yourself locked below decks slaving over dull exercises on a regular basis, something is wrong. It's time to take a field trip—a proper field trip, armed with field guides, notebooks, and clear learning goals (see next chapter, *Top Field Trips in the Caribbean and How to Make the Most of Them*). Move your classroom to the foredeck or the beach occasionally. Spice up your child's learning with fun exercises in a context your child can relate to. If your learning program calls for writing a fictional story, great! Challenge your child to write a pirate story based on your sailing area with him or herself as one of the characters. Linking subjects is another way to make learning fun. The pirate story could be set against the backdrop of a certain period in history, and it could sneak in a little math with a problem leading to the location of the hidden treasure chest. Another example is to collect and identify shells, and then incorporate them in an art project. The list can go on and on.

Just remember: if you treat learning as a heavy chore, your children will echo this attitude and everyone will suffer. On the other hand, if you can establish a playful yet disciplined spirit and stimulate natural curiosity, learning will become an accepted part of your day and one of the richest aspects of the cruising experience.

The world is your classroom

Share the Load

Too often, Dad is the captain with Mom doing everything else: childcare, cooking, and, last but not least, teaching. A certain degree of division of labor is natural, but too much can put unfair strain on either partner. With both parents sharing the teaching load to at least some degree, children can benefit from the strengths of each and from two different teaching styles. Not only that, they are more likely to accept education as a whole-family endeavor, just as the cruise should be a whole-family adventure.

Stop Worrying!

Just thinking about taking over your children's schooling can be intimidating, much like sailing away to unfamiliar waters. Don't get put off by doubts or by land-bound naysayers. Countless families report that cruising with children is the best thing they have ever done, emphasizing the family time and eye-opening experiences their children benefit from. Many also report that their children successfully streamline back into schools when the time comes, and often find themselves academically ahead of their peers.

The truth is that cruising on a well-maintained boat can be safer and healthier than staying on land. Consider highway safety or the germ breeding ground that schools can be. Similarly, homeschooling that is based on sound research and focused on clear goals can supersede what any walled classroom could ever offer. The hardest thing is making the decision to go in the first place. After that, you will find that everything falls into place. Your children will enjoy the experience of a lifetime with the people who count most: their parents, and the lessons learned will guide them for a lifetime.

Chapter 8

Top Field Trips in the Caribbean and How to Make the Most of Them

Kids learn (and remember what they learn) best when they are interested, active, and involved. So take a field trip and kindle the fire of your child's curiosity: see a volcano in action, hold a baby turtle, or explore centuries of history on your own two feet.

A field trip is a great way to link formal education with real-life experiences. The problem with formal learning alone is that it is often too abstract to truly captivate children. The problem with a casual field trip, on the other hand, is that it remains an isolated experience without a link to the big picture. That is why a good field trip should be the middle of three steps. First, comes the preparation. Have your children list what they know (or think they know) about the topic. Read background information to learn more and dispel any misconceptions. If you pack the right books, you can read while underway from one anchorage to the next (the books suggested below are all slim volumes aimed at readers in grades one to four). Generate a checklist of points to observe and questions to answer during the field trip. A thorough checklist will turn your child into a focused researcher rather than a casual tourist.

Next, during the field trip, have your children take notes that answer their own questions as well as the guiding questions listed. Finally, follow up afterwards with a small project that reinforces the lesson. This could be a simple journal entry, a fictional story inspired by the field trip, or a hand-made "Kids' Field Guide to Volcanoes / Turtles / Plantations of the Caribbean." The idea is to reconcile the child's previous knowledge with the new and to build connections to academic subjects where possible. So let's get going!

Volcano Field Trip

Guiding Question: What are the forces at work behind a volcano?

Locations: Sulphur Springs (St. Lucia), Soufrière (St. Vincent), Saint-Pierre (Martinique)

Suggested Reading: *Volcanoes!* by Anne Schreiber (National Geographic Kids, 2008) or *The Magic School Bus Blows its Top* by Gail Herman (Scholastic, 1996).

Our planet is not simply a lump of rock but an active, changing, dynamic ball of energy. (A little like our kids!) For too many children, this concept is too abstract to really internalize—but not if you visit a site like Sulphur Springs (St. Lucia) where you can see boiling, bubbling mud, or Soufrière (St. Vincent) where you can hike up and peer into a steaming crater. Guides or park information boards can help you turn the spectacle into a comprehensive lesson in Earth Science.

Saint-Pierre (Martinique) is a fascinating site because it shows the destructive power of a volcanic eruption. Ruins still dot the town and the museum there does a good job documenting the 1902 event. If you are sailing in the vicinity of Montserrat, that would be another chance to observe volcanic activity, though many cruisers avoid the island due to reported problems such as ash clogging engine exhausts.

Prepare with a book that covers types of volcanoes, lava, and eruptions, and the environmental and social impacts of volcanoes. During the field trip, note the details of your particular volcano. What type is it? Children can sketch what they see and add subsurface features using their reading as a guide. Follow up by making your own "Field Guide to Sulphur Springs." This lesson can be extended to consider the Caribbean as a whole: Which islands were created by volcanic activity (Montserrat, for instance) and which were not (Antigua)?

Turtle Field Trip

Guiding Question: How can we protect migratory sea animals?

Locations: Old Hegg Turtle Sanctuary (Bequia); Tobago Cays

Suggested Reading: *Turtle: Watch Me Grow* by Lisa Magloff (DK Publishing, 2006).

Many sea turtles call the Caribbean home or pass through in their vast migrations. Most species are endangered due to factors such as beach development, entrapment in fishing nets, or predation of eggs. A field trip to a place where you are likely to see turtles can be an excellent opportunity not only to learn more about this interesting animal in particular, but also about environmental conservation as a whole.

On Bequia's windward shore, former fisherman "Brother" King has established a turtle sanctuary where you can study turtles up close. Mr. King is very personable and enjoys educating visitors. Although the scientific jury is out as to whether captive-reared turtles stand a better chance of survival than wild turtles (suggesting that efforts to help would be better targeted at protecting nesting beaches), the sanctuary demonstrates the "value" of turtles to both visitors and locals and therefore garners sympathy for the cause. An article that considers the effectiveness of the sanctuary can be found at: http://www.caribbeancompass.com/turtleok.htm. During the field trip, children can list, describe, and even sketch different species, ask about tracking turtles, and inquire about conservation efforts.

The Tobago Cays are a reliable location to view wild sea turtles: one grassy area off Baradal Island is a sea turtle reserve, although I had more

61

The turtle sanctuary on Bequia

luck spotting turtles while snorkeling over sandy patches nearby. Keep your distance and note the turtles' features, activities, and pattern of movement. Afterwards, follow up with a report on turtles or a "Kids' Field Guide to Turtles of the Caribbean," or design a turtle-themed *Chutes and Ladders*-style survival game.

Columbus Landing Field Trip

Guiding Question: What were the consequences of Columbus' "discovery?"

Locations: San Salvador (Bahamas), Cockburn Town (Grand Turk), Sainte-Marie (Guadeloupe)

Suggested Reading: *The Story of Columbus* by Anita Ganeri (Dorling Kindersley, 2001) or *Who Was Christopher Columbus?* by Bonnie Bader (Grosset and Dunlap, 2013).

Too often, Columbus' "discovery" of the New World is presented as if it were an isolated act. In fact, his arrival set a series of events in motion that had far-reaching and tragic consequences, especially from the perspective of indigenous populations. A visit to one of Columbus' landing sites can be the starting point for a broad-reaching inquiry.

Historians do not agree on the location of Columbus' first landfall in the New World, and several places claim that distinction. Based on Columbus' description, his route across the Atlantic, and backwards calculations from other islands, many believe that Europeans first touched the New World on Watlings Island (renamed San Salvador) in the Bahamas. Others argue that Cat Island, Samana Cay, and Grand Turk are also candidates. Today, monuments stands on these and other, confirmed landing spots from later journeys (including Sainte-Anne, Guadeloupe).

Prepare for the field trip with background reading on Columbus and his four journeys. What were his goals and motives? How did he navigate? During the field trip, find the context of that particular site. Is it a confirmed or a contested landing spot? During which of his four journeys did Columbus land at that point? Where did he stop before this spot and where did he go next? A good follow-up is to study place names of the Caribbean. Some retain indigenous names, while others have European roots, reflecting changing influences.

Indigenous Cultures Field Trip

Guiding Question: Who were the original inhabitants of the Caribbean and what is their story?

Locations: Kalinago Cultural Center (Dominica), Trois-Rivières (Guadeloupe), Carib's Leap (Grenada)

Imagine visiting Japan, but meeting only Koreans. Sounds silly, doesn't it? But that is essentially the case in today's Caribbean, where the original inhabitants have all but disappeared. The word Caribbean comes from the Carib people (although this was a European misunderstanding and not the correct term, much like "American Indian"). The earliest Caribbean settlers were the Siboney, followed later by the Arawak: among them, the Lucayo, Taino, and Kalinago. All perished as a direct or indirect result of

European contact. Some were killed or enslaved, while most succumbed to European diseases. They left few traces behind, and it is worth seeking the remaining sites out as poignant reminders of the past.

On mountainous Dominica, however, a group of Caribs (properly called Kalinago) held out, and their descendants live on today. The fascinating Kalinago Cultural Center is your only chance in the Eastern Caribbean to frame indigenous history within a present-day context. The site is located on windward Dominica; you will need a rental car or hired driver to get there. Tours are conducted by the Kalinago themselves, making the experience unique and unforgettable.

A visit to the Kalinago Cultural Center

If you can't make it to Dominica, visit southern Guadeloupe's Trois-Rivieres, where outstanding examples of rock art have been brought together in a beautiful garden setting. Near Sauteurs in northern Grenada is an excellent visitor's center at Carib's Leap, where the last indigenous islanders jumped off cliffs to their deaths rather than be enslaved. Throughout the Caribbean, you can find examples of rock art, though little else has survived the test of time.

Prepare by reading the history of the Caribs in your Caribbean guidebook. During the field trip, answer questions such as, What distinguished the different indigenous groups from one another? Who are the Kalinago? What was their culture like? Why are most of the indigenous islanders gone? Why does history so often overlook native people? Follow up the visit by writing a more detailed paragraph to be inserted into the history section of your guidebook.

Colonial Superpowers and Plantations Field Trip

Guiding Question: What was life like in the Caribbean two centuries ago?

Locations: English Harbor (Antigua), Fort Napoleon (Terre-de-Haut, Les Saintes), Brimstone Hill (St. Kitts), Fort Shirley (Dominica), Chateau Murat (Marie-Galante), Belmont Estate (Grenada)

Suggested Reading: *Now Let Me Fly* by Dolores Johnson (Macmillan, 1993). A fictional story of a young girl stolen into slavery and taken to the New World. Despite its North American setting, the story provides a good view into plantation life and slavery.

Early Spanish explorers quickly passed by the outer islands on their quest to find riches in the Greater Antilles and the Americas. However, the French, English, and Dutch quickly recognized and exploited the agricultural potential of the "West Indies." They established plantations using slave labor, growing spices and sugar and distilling rum. Economic and political rivalry between the superpowers on the other side of the Atlantic spilled over into the Caribbean, where forts were built to protect the fiercely guarded territories.

Today, stone fortifications dot nearly every island. Several historic plantations are also open for viewing, some of them as ruins (such as Chateau Murat on Marie-Galante), others still operating (such as the Belmont Estate on Grenada). The list above is by no means complete; nearly every island has historic sites you can visit.

Prepare for your field trip by reading and discussing Caribbean history as related in your guidebook. This can turn into a lesson on European history since many islands changed hands as a result of wars and treaties written in a seemingly arbitrary manner so far away. Sometimes, slavery was abolished under French occupation but re-established under the English! During the field trip, children should take notes on key dates, including dates when the fort or plantation changed hands and the outside events influencing them. What was life like in that era, for settlers and slaves? What interests were being fought over? What was grown on this island? What was the pattern of colonial trade? Consider who writes history and whether there is such a thing as a neutral opinion.

Follow up by writing a historical fiction story from the point of view of a plantation worker, settler, or soldier. Students can pick a real event as the background for the fictional story.

This is only a short list of suggested field trips, but it should give you many ideas as to how to turn a casual visit into a valuable learning experience. Not only will your children gain a deeper impression of the Caribbean, they will also be able to make wider connections when back in school.

Recording it all

Chapter 9

Photo Essays

A photo essay is a great way to make learning fun instead of a chore. All your child needs is a camera, a subject of focus, a notepad, an area in which to roam, and presto—they're off on an interesting learning adventure. In essence, a photo essay is really just an illustrated essay. The student will still need to collect, arrange, and present information in an organized way. He or she will still be tasked with writing sections of text, but the photo part of the assignment infuses the enterprise with new life.

I learned this in our time in Panama, where so many wonderful subjects presented themselves to us that even field trips began to feel ordinary. So we tried a photo essay and hit a gold mine. Why? One reason is the chance to get out and about. Another is the student's excitement about being entrusted with the camera. Usually, it's the parents carrying it around; now the kids get their turn.

A camera literally encourages the photographer to look at things from multiple angles. Maybe that's why photo essays are especially well suited to tackling subjects with strong interdisciplinary potential, because one shot can capture several issues at once. Take, for example, the Panama Canal. A single photo of a modern freighter passing through the locks can be a starting point for history (early trade routes, building of the canal), technology (engineering of the canal), science/environment (impact of canal on surrounding rainforest), or current events (geopolitics, world shipping routes). The only danger is trying to tackle too much at once, so remember to keep things focused. A photo essay can cover any subject, whether it's *Our Day at Brimstone Hill Fortress* or *How to Catch a Fish*.

The photo shoot is only one part of the process—one that gives the project momentum. Afterwards, the student still has to organize the work and write blocks of text to go with the pictures. The beauty of this is that the text takes on the form of captions, which can be as brief or detailed as you wish. These are essentially the paragraphs of a multi-paragraph essay. But unlike a regular essay, the writing is automatically broken up into easily managed sections. Thus the writing part of the assignment is much less intimidating.

Photo essays can do much more than just develop writing skills. Photography is an art form that encourages students to consider things like composition, color, and light. There's also the IT side: using software to drop photos into text or a pamphlet format. You can also aim for a movie or PowerPoint presentation. Just be careful, since the technology side can be addictive for some kids and overly time-consuming for others. I personally prefer the simple photo/text format, at least when the main goal is to achieve an understanding of a new subject rather than the makings of a presentation.

Like any written essay, a photo essay needs to find an audience. Post it on your family's travel blog, share it with friends, or present it to Grandma on your next visit. It doesn't have to reach the world, just a few appreciative parties. Last but not least, a photo essay can also become a keepsake of special times in special places. So why not give it a try?

Chapter 10

What About Social Skills?

Thinking of heading out for a longer cruise? One of the common concerns parents have is that their children will be isolated from their peers and thus unable to develop healthy social skills. I worried about it, too, before setting off on our first sailing adventure. But now that we've sailed halfway around the world and lived aboard our thirty-four foot sloop for four years, I can assure you that the family adventure of a lifetime awaits—and it's one you can share with like-minded parents of like-minded children.

Starting out is often the hardest part. Each of our two sailing sabbaticals started with a month or two of minimal contact with other sailing families. But there are families with children of all ages out cruising in all parts of the world, and you will find them, especially once you get to a popular cruising area or on track with a major cruising route. The Bahamas are one such place, and Panama at New Year's is another hot spot where you'll find dozens of Pacific-bound sailors congregating to transit the canal. You'll find cruising families throughout the Eastern Caribbean, as well. We made close friends with several sailing families and stayed together for weeks and even months at a time. One family was our constant companion on a southbound trip along the islands of the Eastern Caribbean, while another was our buddy boat on the northbound leg—all the way north to New York! (Later, when we crossed the Pacific, we sailed off and on with a close group of families for nearly three years and thousands of miles.)

Sailing kids

Sailing kids play together on beaches and on the boats; they do field trips together and even have sleepovers—just like kids at home. On passages, they chat on the radio (VHF and SSB). All in all, the cruising scene can be much more social than people imagine. Of course, it helps to keep your cruising plans flexible to match other families' schedules. We seemed to go through phases: at times, we had a lot of social contact with sailing families. At other times, we did not have another family nearby, so we focused back on our own family time, which was nice, too.

So the answer is no, sailing children are not too isolated to develop healthy social skills. In fact, I believe that many sailing kids develop stronger social skills than they do at home because friends are such an appreciated "commodity." Our son was very shy when we started our second cruise and wouldn't initiate contact with other children without our help. Soon, however, he was comfortable meeting and playing with new acquaintances—even kids with whom he didn't share a common language. They'd quickly learn a few words of each other's language and would be playing like old friends in no time. It is true that there are many more preschool and elementary age children out cruising with their families than middle and high school age kids, but even the latter seem to have a sixth sense when it comes to finding playmates.

After months of observing harmonious interactions between sailing kids, I started to wonder whether they might end up lacking conflict resolution skills. After all, conflict resolution is a social skill that is constantly called upon in a school setting, where there are inevitably clashes of one kind or another. Sailing kids experience fewer direct conflicts because they usually socialize in smaller groups with more parental supervision. Then I took a closer look and realized that sailing kids develop conflict resolution skills at least as well as (and possibly even better than) their peers back home. They deal with conflict in a different way: by learning to avert trouble at a much earlier point that most school children do. They want to enjoy time with other kids, not get aggravated. Most sailing kids we know are very considerate and accommodating. They see friendship for what it should be: something to be nurtured and protected. If only all kids and adults learned this lesson early on!

Generally, sailing kids are also more adept at mixing with a wide age range of children than "regular" kids are. In a normal school setting, children primarily deal with kids of their own age. Sailing children learn to socialize with younger and older kids, too. They learn patience, leadership, and acceptance, and they are challenged to find creative solutions to make play across age ranges fun. Sailing kids also have contact with local children along the way, in both formal and informal settings. It's often possible to arrange a day / a week / a month at a local school so that sailing kids can experience what it is like to sit at a desk, go to recess, eat a group lunch, and perhaps move to specialty areas with art or sports equipment.

Alas, many landlubbers seem to cultivate a medieval world view. We are warned, just as Columbus was warned, that sailing away will be the social equivalent of falling off the edge of the world. But those who dare venture beyond the horizon with their children will find what we did—a new world, waiting to be discovered.

Chapter 11

The Voyages of Christopher Columbus

This chapter is one of ten learning units detailed in my book, *Lesson Plans Ahoy: Hands-On Learning for Sailing Children and Home Schooling Sailors.* That book covers the topic of homeschooling aboard in a comprehensive way and is a great resource for long-term cruisers.

This unit is broken into four parts, followed by a section called *Age-Appropriate Adaptations.* That's where you'll find tips on tailoring the unit to suit children of various age groups. The advantage of this approach is that several children can focus on the same unit at the same time, while each approaches it from his or her own level.

One could write hundreds of pages on Columbus and the Age of Discovery. Why did Columbus sail west? How did he plan his voyage? What was his voyage like? What did he do after his 1492 transatlantic voyage? This unit summarizes key points about the explorer and the era he lived in. This is a comprehensive unit that can easily fill several weeks. On the other hand, one can condense it or focus on a particular section. The text is written so that young students can read most passages alone. Parents can read aloud and adapt the text and corresponding activities for younger children. At the end of this chapter, you will find a number of suggestions for enrichment. It may help to illustrate this chapter through one of the recommended books listed in the *Resources* section.

Overview

This unit is divided into four sections. Students will gain a deeper understanding of the subject when they study not only Columbus' 1492 journey, but also its historic context and its consequences. However, parents may choose to emphasize certain sections more than others depending on age and time considerations.

Sections 1 and 2 contain the basic information on Columbus' background and his 1492 journey. Sections 3 and 4 follow up with the fascinating second, third, and fourth voyages and the consequences of his discoveries. The text of this chapter can be simplified for young children. Parents can first read through it themselves and mark with a highlighter those passages they will read aloud or the passages that their children can read. Only very advanced students will read an entire section in one sitting; most likely, they will divide the work over a number of days and take time between for the recommended activities and assignments. Students may choose just one assignment or work through all of them as a series. While reading the sections below, it is helpful to refer to the maps frequently (several are included).

Following the main body of this unit, you will find detailed instructions for Age-Appropriate Adaptations of all the materials. This will guide parents in tailoring the unit to fit each child's level.

Section 1: The Man and His Times

In 1492, Columbus crossed the ocean blue. This simple rhyme hides many fascinating facts about the man and his times. How did he cross the ocean blue? How did he even get the idea? What made him attempt a feat that many people thought was impossibly dangerous? What were the consequences of his crossing? We shall soon see that there is much more to his story than simply "crossing the ocean blue."

Columbus Landfall National Park, Grand Turk

The man we call Christopher Columbus was born in Genoa (in today's Italy) in 1451. His real (Italian) name was Cristoforo Colombo. Since the first English book about him used the Latin version of his name, he is usually called Christopher Columbus by English speakers.

Genoa was at that time a city-state: something like a tiny country of its own, because Italy was not yet united into one country as it is today. Genoa was a lively trading city with many sailing ships coming and going. Although his father was a weaver, Columbus went to sea at about age ten and sailed on many trips around the Mediterranean. In 1476, he joined a trading ship that was headed out of the Mediterranean and into the Atlantic. However, the ship was attacked by the French and the crew was shipwrecked. Columbus survived by swimming and resting on a floating piece of wood until he came to the shore in Portugal. This near-disaster had an important influence on Columbus' career. Columbus went to join his brother Bartholomeo, who was working as a chart maker in Lisbon, the capital city. In Portuguese, the name Christopher appears as Cristovão or Cristoforo, and Columbus as Colón, Colom, or Colomo.

It is interesting and important to realize what the European world was like at that time. Columbus lived in an era of transition between the end of the Medieval period and the beginning of Renaissance times in Europe (neither era has exact start or end dates) when Portugal was at one edge of the known world. As a boy, Columbus was fascinated by Marco Polo's adventurous travel tales (dating from around 1300) describing the wonders of Asia.

People in Europe were willing to pay large amounts of money for spices, silk, and tea brought from what they called the Orient: India, China, and Japan. But in 1453, the Ottoman Turks captured Constantinople (today's Istanbul, in Turkey), which until then was the capital of the Byzantine Empire. Turkish control of this important city made products from the East even more expensive and harder to obtain. Therefore, European countries like Spain and Portugal wanted to find their own routes to the riches of the Orient, and to do this they looked across the sea. One important person in this effort was Prince Henry the Navigator (Infante Dom Henrique, a son of the Portuguese king) who established a navigation center and sent explorers south along the coast of Africa.

Columbus married a Portuguese woman (Dona Felipa Perestrello é Moniz) and moved to Porto Santo, a small island near Portuguese-owned Madeira. There, they were on the edge of the Ocean Sea. This was what people called what they thought was one, great, connected ocean touching Europe, India, and Asia. In a way, they were right, because the Atlantic, Indian, and Pacific Oceans are all connected in the Southern Hemisphere. Europeans didn't imagine there was another great continent–the Americas–in between Europe and Asia.

Columbus' father-in-law had a strong interest in the Ocean Sea. He even had a collection of unusual plants and wood that had washed ashore, presumably from unknown lands across the sea. Columbus also had heard some strange stories of islands and people who came from across the Ocean Sea. All this inspired Columbus' curiosity and formed part of the proof he eventually gathered to gain support for a voyage west.

Columbus thought it should be possible to reach the Orient by traveling west across the Ocean Sea, and calculated the distance to be about 5,000 kilometers. During his many sailing trips–maybe even as far north as Ireland and Iceland–Columbus observed that the prevailing winds came from the west at high latitudes, while in Madeira and the Canaries, the wind was usually from the east. Therefore, he reasoned, he should be able to catch favorable winds both across and back over the Ocean Sea. He called his idea of sailing west to establish trading posts "the Enterprise of the Indies."

At that time, few educated people thought the earth was a flat disc that ships could sail off the edge of. This is a misconception we often read in books. Scholars understood that Earth is round. Some even developed a way of estimating its size, though the results varied greatly. Several mathematicians calculated the distance west to the Orient to be about 15,000 kilometers. No ship of the day could carry enough supplies and sail so far. Columbus disagreed with their estimate and said the distance was only 5,000 kilometers. The mathematicians were right about the distance, but in a way, Columbus was right, too. There was indeed land 5,000 kilometers west of Europe, but nobody suspected that it was a new continent later named America!

In 1484, Columbus managed to gain an audience with Portugal's King Juan II and tried to convince him to pay for the Enterprise of the Indies. Columbus failed to convince the king and the royal advisors: they disagreed with his estimate of the distance and found Columbus too boastful and demanding. When Columbus tried to convince the king again in 1488, he was too late: explorer Bartolomeu Dias had just returned from a passage around the southern tip of Africa, rounding the Cape of Good Hope and entering the Indian Ocean. That meant that Portugal had no need of a dangerous route to the west now that they found–and controlled–a route around Africa.

So Columbus had to try elsewhere, and, after his wife died, he traveled to Spain with his young son Diego. In Spain, his name was again changed: there, he was known as Cristoval or Cristóbal Colón. He and his son were taken in by monks with an interest in navigation who encouraged his idea. Columbus was eventually granted an audience with the rulers of a newly united Spain, King Ferdinand and Queen Isabella. They took interest in his idea, especially since their Portuguese rivals were ahead of Spain in finding a way to the Orient. However, their advisors disagreed with Columbus' distance calculations. At the same time, Spain was involved in a long, costly war with the Moors (Muslims from North Africa) who occupied the southern part of Spain. The monarchs could not pay for an expedition to the Orient before this war ended. Columbus waited six long years to be able to "sell" his idea. Finally, in 1492, the war was won, and Columbus was granted another audience, but again failed to convince the queen's advisors.

Discouraged, Columbus prepared to leave Spain and try his luck in France when Queen Isabella had him called back. One of Columbus' supporters had convinced Isabella that for a small investment of only three ships, Spain could possibly gain great riches if Columbus succeeded. Even if he was very demanding (Columbus wanted a huge percentage of all profits and hereditary rights that would pass to his children), it was a still a good deal for the Queen. She agreed. At last, he had a sponsor!

Now Columbus was finally ready to cross the ocean blue. For Europe, it would be an exciting new era of exploration, expansion, and conquest; for America (and later, Africa), it was to be a tragic era of exploitation.

Section 1 Assignment

Students can try to rewrite history by writing a persuasive letter from Columbus to Portugal's King Juan II dated 1484. That is the monarch who rejected the Enterprise of the Indies because Columbus was not convincing enough, too demanding in his terms, and too boastful in his presentation. List all the reasons why Portugal would benefit from Columbus' voyage. Students should also detail what Columbus expects to receive as a reward. This serves as a good review of Section 1 and a means to practice persuasive writing.

Section 2: The 1492 Voyage

The ocean was a large, unknown blank space on the map and few believed that it could be crossed safely. For sailors in the fifteenth century, it was as much a New World as the Americas would soon prove to be.

Luckily, the Spanish coastal city of Palos owed the monarchs a debt and was therefore required to supply two ships for Columbus: these were the Niña and Pinta. Columbus chartered a third ship, the Santa Maria; she was the biggest of the three at about twenty meters. Within a few months, Columbus had his crew and ships ready and set off on his voyage at last. The monarchs promised Columbus ten percent of any profits gained, rule of any new lands he discovered, and the title "Admiral of the Ocean Sea."

It probably isn't true that Columbus could hardly convince sailors to join his daring voyage. He was able to get a full crew of mostly experienced sailors from Palos, about ninety men in all. Even though he was making a trip into unknown territory and expected to find some new places on the way to the Orient, Columbus didn't bring any soldiers or many weapons on his first trip. He was very religious and wanted to bring his Christian religion to other people, but he did not bring any priests on the first trip, either. This suggests that exploration was his main purpose.

On August 3, 1492, Columbus led his ships out of Palos and set a course first for the Canary Islands, a passage of about a week. Most transatlantic sailors today follow the same route. In the Canaries, he completed work on his ships and took on food and water. He had the Niña's rig changed to make her a square-rigger instead of a lateen rig (a triangular sail more like modern boats) because he predicted downwind sailing. Then, on September 6, 1492, the three ships departed the island of Gomera for the ocean crossing.

Columbus the Sailor and Navigator

As we have seen, Columbus was already a well-traveled sailor who had made many observations about the Ocean Sea. He had worked as a mapmaker with his brother in Lisbon and spoke several languages, skills that helped on this trip. It is interesting to remember that he was Genoese, even though he worked for Spain and with a Spanish crew. This would bring him problems in stressful times when the Spanish crew looked for any excuse they could to disagree with their captain.

For navigation, Columbus mostly used dead reckoning, rough estimates of currents, and magnetic courses (not a corrected, or true, course). Dead reckoning means that he charted his day's course and the distance covered to find where he was. For example, if he sailed west all day and calculated that the ship covered one hundred miles, then he would draw a line west one hundred miles. [1]

Columbus also had two instruments for celestial navigation (using measurements of the sun, moon, and stars): a simple quadrant and an astrolabe. Both of these instruments are similar to a sextant and measure the height of the sun, moon, or North Star above the horizon. Columbus tried making a few celestial observations during his voyages across the Ocean Sea but was not successful in reliably establishing his location in this way.

From his experience, Columbus developed a good sense for currents, wind, and weather. He had a rough map showing Japan (called "Cipango") west of Europe, with a few imaginary islands drawn in between. [2] Columbus proved to be an excellent navigator who safely brought his ships through reef-filled waters, as we shall see. Today, sailors would hardly imagine leaving land without modern navigational tools. What tools do we have today that Columbus did not?

Columbus was one of the first ship's captains to keep a log, or written record of his voyage, including estimated positions and notes about events. This document has not survived but a partial copy made after Columbus' death did, providing many important and interesting details about his first journey.

---

[1] Strictly speaking, dead reckoning does not allow for leeway. Dead reckoning also leaves out any effect of currents that push the boat. Columbus was able to work surprisingly well combining dead reckoning with good judgement of currents. Later he was able to find the same places using his own records.

[2] The circa 1481 Toscanelli chart. This Italian chart maker was one of the first to use a grid of latitude and longitude over the known world, with Europe on the right side of the sheet, the Ocean Sea in the middle, and Asia on the left.

The Nina and the Pinta

The 1492 Voyage

Three ships sailed into unknown waters on the Enterprise of the Indies. Try to imagine what it would be like to sail while keeping in sight of two other ships at all times. The ships needed each other for safety; if they became separated, the crews would have no way to find each other again. It must have been very tiring to watch out for each other for weeks at a time. The Niña and Pinta were faster than the Santa Maria, which meant they often had to slow down and let Columbus catch up. By day, the ships would spread out as far as the horizon, but by night, they made sure to come together again.

The ships had a lower deck that was mostly used for storage. The crew would sleep on the open deck. There were no bunks; sailors just lay down wherever they could find a spot. Only Columbus had a tiny private cabin, something like a hut on the deck. Food was simple, mostly preserved goods like hardtack (a type of biscuit) and salted meat. Catching fresh fish was a welcome change to a sailor's diet! The crew cooked on a special sand-lined firebox kept on the deck.

The journey began slowly with weak wind, and Columbus and his men went through a number of mood swings throughout the voyage (much like modern sailors). There were times when everything seemed to go well and other times when the crew was close to mutiny. Days and weeks passed, and several false clues and sightings of land wore down the crew's patience and trust in Columbus.

Columbus kept two records of their progress: his secret version, in which he estimated their position as exactly as possible, and a second version for the benefit of the crew. This version made their distance from Spain seem less, because Columbus thought that the men would be afraid to know exactly how far they really were from home.

The crew eagerly watched for signs of land. They saw a tropical bird just a week after departure and thought land could not be far. Patches of Sargasso weed again tricked them into thinking that land was near. They made the same mistake with weather observations: "It started to rain without wind, which is a sure sign of land," Columbus wrote (Fuson, Pg. 64). On Sept. 21, still twenty days from landfall, they "saw a whale, which is another sign of land, for whales always stay near the coast" (Fuson, Pg. 66). On October 7, they saw large flocks of birds and thought they must be close to land. Alas, they were witnessing birds on migration, flying south for the winter. Imagine how the crew's faith in the Enterprise of the Indies was tested by this ongoing guessing game of "Are we there yet?"

Even the captains of the Niña and Pinta were beginning to have their doubts. Columbus convinced them to sail on for three more days, and just in time, on October 12, the fleet finally sighted land. After thirty-three days at sea, they had arrived in the Bahamas and in a new world. Columbus went ashore on the small island he named San Salvador. He planted a flag to claim it for Spain. Now Columbus could really call himself "Admiral of the Ocean Sea, Viceroy and Governor of lands that he may discover."

Soon the Spaniards made contact with the native Lucayo people, a sub-group of the Arawak natives spread across the Caribbean. Columbus, thinking he had reached the far edge of the Indies, called them Indians, a term that was then widely–if incorrectly–applied to indigenous people throughout the Americas.

Columbus thought this island (called Guanahani by its inhabitants) must lie at the end of an archipelago leading to Cipango (Japan). It is perhaps strange that Columbus should think he was at the edge of lands belonging to a great Asian Emperor and, at the same time, claim them for Spain. However, the land seemed nearly empty, settled only by "primitive" people, and was therefore fair game as far as the fifteenth century European mind was concerned.

Experts disagree about exactly where Columbus made his first landfall. Based on Columbus' description, his route across the Atlantic, and backwards calculations from his later discoveries, many believe it to be Watlings Island (which was actually renamed San Salvador in 1925). However, other historians argue that Cat Island, Samana Cay, and Grand Turk (of the Turks & Caicos) are other possibilities.

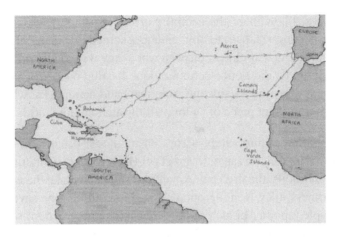

Route of Columbus' First Voyage

Columbus was excited to see that some of the "Indians" wore gold jewelry. Through sign language, they showed that gold could be found on larger islands nearby, and soon Columbus set off again. The indigenous people made important contributions to Columbus' explorations. They had dugout canoes and knew their waters very well. Their instructions led Columbus from island to island and eventually, just as they had said, to very large islands farther south and west. They also described islands of the Lesser Antilles farther south through sign language and "sketched" charts with beans as islands. These proved extremely useful to Columbus on this and later voyages.

At sea, the men thought only of land; once on land, they seemed to mainly think about finding gold. After navigating the shallows of the Bahamas–an admirable feat for a captain without detailed charts and ships that drew two meters of water–the fleet sailed on to Cuba, and then to an island Columbus named La Isla Española (today's Hispaniola, shared by

Haiti and the Dominican Republic). Along the way, they made repeated, mostly peaceful, contact with indigenous people. Columbus was furious when the captain of the Pinta, Martín Alonso Pinzón, disobeyed orders and sailed away to Great Inagua Island, following up on rumors of gold. He soon was to cause Columbus more headaches.

Columbus thought he was in Asia and interpreted everything accordingly. Place names, like Cibao (the central part of Hispaniola), sounded close enough to Cipango (Japan) to him, and he assumed that many plants were Oriental spices such as cinnamon even when they were oddly different. At the same time, he did notice certain unique local goods, such as tobacco (unknown at that time outside the Americas) and hammocks, which soon became an important piece of sailor's kit throughout the world.

Ironically, after sailing safely across an unknown ocean and countless shoals, the Santa Maria ran onto a reef off Hispaniola on Christmas night. In calm conditions, the tired helmsman let a ship's boy take the wheel, and in the darkness, they went aground. The ship could not be saved. Local Taino people (another branch of the Arawak language group) helped the crew save everything they could. Columbus, an extremely religious man, took this as a sign that God wanted him to establish a settlement at this location. Thirty volunteers, tempted by the promise of gold around every corner, stayed to man the new fort called La Navidad. The Niña, now with Columbus and extra crew aboard, headed back to Spain with news of their incredible feat. By chance, they encountered renegade Captain Pinzón aboard the Pinta and continued on together.

Their return journey, starting at the height of winter on January 16, 1493, was to be much more difficult than the outgoing trip. Columbus turned his ships north until they reached westerly winds to bring them back to Spain. However, a series of terrible storms separated the ships and had the crew praying for their lives. Columbus even wrote a summary of his discovery and threw it overboard in a cask: in the event of sinking, he was desperate that someone find out about his great achievement.

The Niña and her crew survived the storms and eventually stopped on the island of Santa Maria in the Azores in mid-February. As if he had not already been tested enough, Columbus now had the problem that half of his company were jailed when they went ashore the Portuguese-owned island to go to church! He did manage to clear this up and sail on, but encountered yet another violent storm that nearly pushed the Niña against a dangerous section of the Portuguese coast. Columbus made another emergency stop in Lisbon, and eventually sailed on to Palos in Spain.

Martín Pinzón and the Pinta had arrived in Spain just before Columbus. As first to arrive, he had the chance to upstage Columbus. Pinzón tried to see the King and Queen first, but they refused him an audience and waited for Columbus. Pinzón, disappointed and ill from the difficult journey, died within a month. Columbus made quite a splash with his parade of tropical birds, Taino natives, [1] and samples of gold. He had earned his title of Admiral of the Ocean Sea and proven his many critics wrong. He was sure he had opened the door to Oriental riches for the Queen and King of Spain. In fact, he had discovered a New World, though no one yet suspected it. This is evident in the fact that the monarchs were willing to give him power over all new lands he discovered–if they had suspected a huge new continent rich in natural resources, they never would have been so generous!

Columbus' discovery was to bring many riches to Spain but many changes to the known world as well, many of them tragic for the people and creatures of the Americas. It was not long before Columbus was planning his next ocean crossing.

Section 2 Activity & Assignment

Activity: Dead reckoning. Columbus' primary means of navigation was dead reckoning (DR). He plotted the course steered (using magnetic headings, not corrected true headings) over the distance he estimated his ship traveled. Do this with your own positions over a period of time and see how your DR position and actual position compare. Then list other factors that influence a boat's movement over the sea that DR does not consider.

---

[1] Accounts differ, but it seems that about ten Taino went to Spain with Columbus. Few, if any, went voluntarily, and not all survived the journey. Others returned to the Caribbean on Columbus' second journey.

Assignment: Make a collage, comic strip, or other artwork depicting Columbus' first journey, or another series of significant events relating to the Age of Discovery.

Section 3: Columbus' Subsequent Voyages

With his 1492 voyage, Columbus discovered much about the Ocean Sea. It is true that Vikings had already crossed the ocean five hundred years before Columbus; however, they did not spread news of their discoveries or maintain contact with the new world. The Viking settlement in Vinland (today's Newfoundland) was eventually abandoned and forgotten. In contrast, news of Columbus' route west spread quickly. A summary of his trip was published and sold widely, so that people throughout Western Europe could read his amazing story. It is in one of these publications that his name was written as Columbus instead of Colombo or Colón.

Popular history seems to leave his travels at a single year of sailing the ocean blue. In fact, Columbus sailed on three more voyages. These journeys are equally interesting and had a great impact on the New World, which was to be explored, colonized, and exploited at an incredible pace.

The Second Voyage, 1493-1496

The Spanish King and Queen wasted no time in financing a second voyage of totally different character and size. This time Columbus commanded seventeen ships filled with soldiers, priests, settlers—over 1,000 men—in addition to livestock, ready to open the new land for their own use. Europeans were coming to the Americas for good.

After departing Hierro in the Canary Islands in October 1493, Columbus took a more southerly course than he did before–exactly the route followed by modern sailors. Remarkably, he took only twenty-one days to cross the Atlantic, comparable to the speed of many modern sailing vessels. More amazing still, he arrived just where he had wanted: in sight of Dominica and Guadeloupe in the Leeward Islands. The Lucayo had informed him well about which Caribbean islands lay farthest east!

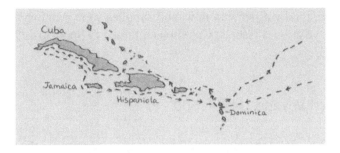

Route of Columbus' Second Voyage

Columbus followed the chain of islands north, naming them as he went. Guadeloupe was named for the church in which he had prayed before his departure in Spain, Antigua for a portrait of the Virgin Mary, and another island for his patron, Saint Christopher (the name of this island is now shortened to St. Kitts). This was probably the zenith of Columbus' happy days as a sailor, leader, and explorer, because a long series of setbacks and failures was soon to set in.

Arriving on Hispaniola in late November, Columbus and his men were shocked to find the small settlement of La Navidad burned and none of the settlers in sight. Soon dead bodies were found and the local chief, who had been friendly to Columbus in 1492, filled in the details. The Spanish settlers had quickly fallen to fighting among themselves, lost the trust of the locals with their demands, and fought with another group of inland natives who killed them all. Columbus abandoned the site and built a new settlement, La Isabela, farther east. The idea was not so much to establish a new colony for Spaniards to move to, but rather a trading post where they could get gold and other valuable Oriental goods.

Columbus left most of the men and supplies to set up La Isabela while he continued his explorations with three ships. They explored the south coast of Cuba and Jamaica, chasing rumors of gold but mostly finding dangerous shoals and sometimes, hostile natives. Eventually, Columbus returned to La Isabela, where he had the difficult job of governing an unruly group of settlers. Many of the Spanish men were unwilling to work hard to make their venture a success and resented Columbus' position as Viceroy (a position with local powers of a king). Conflicts with the locals

87

intensified, gold was slow to flow, and supplies were running low. After a difficult year at La Isabela, Columbus returned to Spain in 1496 to seek more help.

The Third Voyage, 1498-1500

Columbus was to experience new lows during and after his third voyage. Three ships sailed directly to La Isabela with supplies, while three others, led by Columbus, set off on further explorations. After all, they had still not found the Orient itself.

Columbus sailed farther south than ever before, calling at the well-known Cape Verde Islands (off the African coast) before turning west for the Caribbean. The fleet made a fast passage and landfall in Trinidad. While exploring the Gulf of Paria, Columbus thought that the coast in sight was another large island. In fact, it was the continent of South America. Suffering from poor health, Columbus eventually turned north for Hispaniola. He sailed directly across the Caribbean Sea and arrived in Hispaniola almost exactly as intended. Consider what a navigational feat this was! Using only dead reckoning, Columbus connected two separate ends of a chart that he was essentially drawing as he sailed, again covering completely unknown waters and drawing on his faith in himself to reach his chosen destination.

Few celebrated his return. The poor location of La Isabela had been abandoned and a new trading post, Santo Domingo, had been established under the leadership of Columbus' brother, Bartholomeo. However, life there proved no easier than at La Isabela. Soon, Columbus was dealing with a revolt of Spanish settlers who resented his leadership. A new governor (Francisco de Bobadilla) arrived from Spain to take over. Bobadilla immediately exercised his new powers by arresting Columbus and sending him back to Spain, humiliated.

Luckily, Queen Isabella proved a faithful supporter of Columbus and immediately freed him. She even allowed him to keep his grand titles, but, recognizing his weaknesses as a colonial leader, these were now empty of any power. Other people would govern the lands he found; other sailors

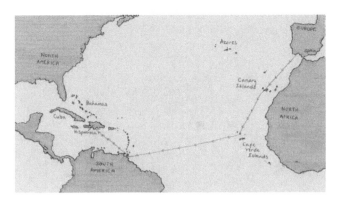

Route of Columbus' Third Voyage

would explore the new coasts he had discovered. However, Columbus was not ready to give up, and managed to convince the crown to finance his fourth, and final, voyage.

The Fourth Voyage, 1502-1504

Columbus, aging and humiliated, was determined to finally find a way through his "Indies" to the Indian Ocean. It was to be an incredible voyage of misadventure and survival. Setting out with four ships from Cadiz in 1502, Columbus made a quick twenty-one day crossing to Martinique and retraced the steps of his second voyage along the Lesser Antilles to the colony at Santo Domingo.

Columbus' vast experience and keen powers of observation told him that a hurricane was approaching. However, the new governor of Santo Domingo ignored his warnings and even refused Columbus entry to the port! In spite of Columbus' forecast, a fleet of thirty ships left port at the end of June, loaded with gold and goods for Spain. Columbus' ships weathered the hurricane well in a nearby river, but more than twenty ships of the treasure fleet were sunk. Most of the gold was lost along with hundreds of lives (among them, Columbus' old enemy, Bobadilla).

Soon, Columbus set off again to look for his route to the west. His ships sailed first along Hispaniola, Jamaica, and Cuba, before moving farther

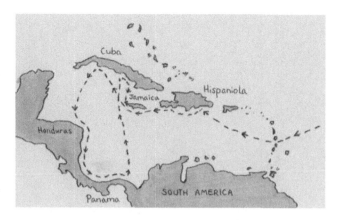

Route of Columbus' Fourth Voyage

west and making the first European sighting of Central America in to-day's Honduras and then Panama, fighting headwinds most of the way. Again, Columbus learned a valuable piece of information from natives. They told him that another ocean lay just over the mountains at this narrow isthmus. Still, Columbus imagined himself to be somewhere on the edge of Asia and did not understand the importance of this information. He sailed on and missed the chance to "discover" the Pacific Ocean and establish the Americas as continents. Perhaps Columbus also missed his chance to have this new continent named after him. Instead, it took the name of Amerigo Vespucci, an Italian mapmaker who sailed to the Gulf of Paria with another expedition. After his work was published, many Europeans attached the name "Amerigo" and eventually "America" to the continents.

As always, the Spanish fleet was guided by its lust for gold, and in a region of Panama they named Veragua, they saw plenty of it. Eager to find its source, Columbus established a base in the Rio Belén, another poor location. Repeating the same cycle of earlier voyages, relations with the locals again turned bad. After several months of trouble, a large number of natives made a coordinated attack on the Spaniards. One ship was abandoned, along with the doomed fort, and Columbus retreated back to Santo Domingo, once again short of achieving his goal.

The remaining three ships were in terrible condition and leaking badly from the attack of their other enemy: teredo shipworms which bored into the wooden ships like termites. One of the ships sank at sea and her men were taken aboard the remaining two. After another storm and desperate pumping, Columbus was forced to beach his sorry fleet in St. Anne's Bay, Jamaica. They were marooned.

One of his men set off in a native canoe and made the dangerous open water passage to Santo Domingo, a brave and incredible feat. However, he was jailed by the unfriendly governor and delayed for over a year! On Jamaica, Columbus again struggled with an unruly crew and clashes with locals. One can only imagine what a humbling, desperate time this must have been for the Admiral of the Ocean Sea. Eventually rescued, Columbus returned to Spain in 1504. He died two years later, never recognizing that his explorations had paved the way to a new continent.

Section 3 Activity & Assignment

Activity: Students should plot Columbus' trips on a chart along with their own route. Do the trails ever intersect? Student can also study the geography of the area around them. What continents, seas, and islands are important? Can the student imagine sailing without a chart?

Assignment: Which of Columbus' voyages do you find most interesting? Students should write an essay or create an artwork that covers the major points of that voyage and the reasons why it is interesting to them.

Section 4: Consequences of Columbus' Voyages

We often say that Columbus discovered America, but of course he only discovered it for Europe. The original discoverers were people who made their way across the Bering Strait from Asia thousands of years earlier. With the arrival of Columbus and mass European colonialism, their continent was changed forever.

Within a few years of Columbus' voyages, explorers forced their way across the Americas, recognizing they were on a new continent and taking its resources for themselves and their kings. Giovanni Caboto (John Cabot) opened North America to his English sponsors in 1497. In 1500, explorer Pedro Cabral "discovered" Brazil and claimed it for Portugal. Vasco Nuñez de Balboa crossed Panama in 1513 to become the first European to sight the Pacific Ocean from the Americas. Hernan Cortez conquered the Aztecs of Mexico in 1521; in 1533, Francisco Pizarro killed the Incan Emperor, bringing that South American civilization to a sudden end.

Columbus said that the natives he encountered were mostly peaceful people living in a simple state as if in the Garden of Eden. However, Spanish efforts to take over the land and convert the indigenous people to Christianity quickly made their world into something more like hell. Together with the fierce Carib people, the Taino lost their land, were forced into slavery, and even actively hunted. (Lucayo, Taino, and Carib are all different groups of native people, together part of the broader Arawak group, inhabiting the Caribbean and the Bahamas at the time of Columbus' journeys.) Those who escaped direct violence–even natives who never saw a European–suffered from diseases like measles and smallpox brought by the Spaniards. Within fifty years, the native population of Hispaniola fell from an estimated 250,000 to only five hundred. One priest, Bartolomé de Las Casas, chronicled the tragic decline of native populations and fought for human rights reforms, but it was too late (see *Resources*, below). The Taino / Arawak natives were nearly "extinct."

Land not taken by the Spanish was soon claimed by the Portuguese, English, and French. They looked beyond gold to plantation agriculture and eventually turned the Caribbean into a massive sugar factory. Because the declining populations of native people were unsuited for such work, the Europeans brought in a new labor force: African slaves. We sailors who explore the Caribbean today see a completely different population from the one originally occupying the area. An entire race was replaced by another, who developed a new, unique culture of their own, with African roots and Caribbean adaptations.

On most islands, the only reminders of native peoples are rock carvings. One exception can be found on the island of Dominica, where hardy Caribs (properly known as Kalinago) took refuge in the mountains and survived. Today, the Kalinago Cultural Center allows visitors a rare view into this culture. Another surviving group, the "Black Caribs" of St. Vincent (so named after the population mixed with escaped slaves) were forcibly relocated to the Honduran island of Roatan in 1797.

Columbus' second and subsequent voyages introduced European livestock and seeds to the New World: these began their own attacks on native populations. Countless species went extinct or became endangered as a result of the intruders. Huge areas of native forest were lost to farmland. Environmental issues we discuss today (extinction, non-native species running out of control, overuse of natural resources) are nothing new. Interestingly, one European import–the horse–was quickly embraced on the mainland by North American tribes.

The New World had its exports to Europe as well. Corn and potatoes were brought back, and the latter became an important part of the European diet. Other imports from the New World were unwelcome, such as the disease syphilis. The unhealthy habit of smoking tobacco quickly spread in the Old World, as well.

Another consequence of Columbus' voyage was its importance for sailors like us. Columbus pioneered a new, optimal route across the open sea, which many of us follow and enjoy today, sailing in the wake of history.

Columbus: Hero or Villain?

For many years, Columbus' story was told in heroic terms. Since 1889, the United States has celebrated Columbus Day as a national holiday. More recently, different points of view have created a more mixed portrait of Columbus and the impact of his voyages. 1492 was an exciting starting point for Europeans, but it was the beginning of the end from the indigenous point of view.

Columbus was an enterprising and adventurous man whose vision allowed him to accomplish what no one dared try before. Many of his decisions and conclusions were based on his religious beliefs. Columbus wanted to convert natives to Christianity while promoting their exploitation as a work force. Although this may seem contradictory to us today, it is consistent with the era in which he lived.

Columbus set into motion an unstoppable series of events with terrible, tragic consequences not only for the native people of the Americas, but also for the African slave force eventually brought in to support colonization. He did not set out to purposely steal or kill, but those were some consequences of his actions. It is known that Columbus personally dealt in slavery in 1496, when he sent three hundred natives to be sold in Spain. However, Queen Isabella objected to slavery and returned those people to the Caribbean. Spain did support a system of *encomiendas,* in which a Spaniard would be given rights over certain natives, from whom he could demand labor or goods, while teaching them Spanish and converting them to Christianity.

Was Columbus a hero or a villain? You will have to decide for yourself.

Section 4 Activity & Assignment

Activity: Students should create a list, diagram, or artwork that depicts the different groups of people, creatures, and lands affected by Columbus' discoveries. They should think about people and the environment on both sides of the Atlantic. Alternatively, students can search maps to find as many places named for Columbus (or versions of his name) as possible.

Assignment: Go back to the simple rhyme we started with: In 1492, Columbus sailed the ocean blue. Students have learned that there is much more to his story than that. Now they should write more lines to complete the rhyme and make it more correctly reflect Columbus' impact on world history, positive and negative.

Age-Appropriate Adaptations

In this section, you will find guidance on how to differentiate, or adapt, this unit for your child. Start with the correct age group, but also glance through the notes for one level younger or older, then mix and match as appropriate.

Self-assessment and reflection are valuable learning tools. They encourage students to think back upon their work and store their new body of knowledge in a meaningful and memorable manner. To that end, a number of self-assessment and reflection questions are listed for each age group. It is not necessary to address all the questions; substitute others as you see fit. Completed assignments and written reflection are useful records to later document student work for a school administration.

Ages 4-6

Young students can do much of the suggested work in some form, but be selective in what you undertake. At this age, the most important concepts to reinforce are the basics of Columbus' explorations, and the fact that history has more than one side. Suggestions for adapting the activities and assignments are listed here. All written assignments should be converted to verbal or role-playing activities.

Section 1 Assignment: Write a persuasive letter from Columbus to Portugal's King Juan II. Obviously there is no need for any written work at this level. However, young students could have fun and reinforce what they have learned by role-playing Columbus' meeting with King Juan II in 1484. They might try one polite and one demanding version of the same exchange.

Section 2 Activity: Practice dead reckoning. If preschool students are to attempt this activity at all, it should be in extremely simplified form. Using a sheet of graph paper and a sketch of the cardinal directions, dictate a series of moves to your child. For example, what if our boat sailed south three boxes, then west ten boxes, etc. Where would we be then? Parents can draw a rough sketch of the boat's geographic area on the paper and have their children advance the boat toward the destination, keeping to the simplest directions possible (whole numbers and basic north/south/west/east steps only).

Section 2 Assignment: Make a collage or comic strip depicting Columbus' first journey. Parents can help students select one episode to represent through the art form of their choice.

Section 3 Activity: Plot Columbus' trips on a chart along with your own. Young children can simply trace and color the map provided and add their own route, perhaps connecting dots provided by parents. This exercise will reinforce the geography of your own trip in the child's mind.

Section 3 Assignment: Which of Columbus' voyages do you find most interesting? One might add, which voyage would the student most like to be a part of and why? This assignment can be carried out verbally or in the form of an art project.

Section 4 Activity: Create a list, diagram, or artwork that depicts the different groups of people, creatures, and lands affected by Columbus' discoveries or search maps to find Columbus-related place names. This age group can omit this activity or do the Columbus name search with parental guidance.

Section 4 Assignment: Extend the rhyme: In 1492, Columbus sailed the ocean blue. Young children develop their language skills through rhymes, so challenge them to find words that rhyme with blue and see if you can come up with any more lines, no matter how silly or off topic they may be!

Self-Assessment and Reflection: Students should review any artwork produced. Ask students what the art represents about this chapter in history, and then pose questions such as:

- Are you pleased with the results of your work? Be specific.

- How did you achieve what you did?

- What did you do especially well? What could you have done better?

- What do you have in common with sailors like Columbus?

What are your differences?

Ages 6-8

Young students can do most of the activities and assignments in this unit in modified form. The most important concepts to reinforce are the basics of Columbus' explorations, and the fact that every story has more than one side. Written assignments can be converted to verbal or role-playing activities, or they can be attempted in list or bullet-point form completed with guidance.

You can work through the text by having an adult read most passages aloud and the child reading selected sections. The reading will go smoothly if you highlight which sections each reader should speak, the parent's part in one color and the student's in another. You may find it necessary to simplify the text or omit some passages.

Section 1 Assignment: Write a persuasive letter from Columbus to Portugal's King Juan II. Students in this age group could prepare a list of important points and role-play the encounter between Columbus and King Juan II. More advanced students might use letter format. They could try one polite and one demanding version of the same message.

Section 2 Activity: Practice dead reckoning. Students ages six to eight should be ready to work with basic or combined cardinal directions (northwest, SSE, etc). The most advanced children in this age bracket might be ready to work with 360° courses. It is unlikely that they will have much appreciation for the concept of true versus magnetic courses or other factors that affect the movement of a boat over the sea.

Section 2 Assignment: Make a collage or comic strip depicting Columbus' first journey. Students should create a series of images to represent Columbus' first journey.

Section 3 Activity: Plot Columbus' trips on a chart along with your own. Point out and define geographic features such as continents, islands, peninsulas, etc. Discuss the idea of the Ocean Sea and look at a modern world map. Roughly sketch the route of Columbus' trips onto relevant sections of your chart. Do you ever intersect his course? Imagine his thoughts as he explored new lands. This exercise will help reinforce your own trip in your child's mind as well as support the history lesson.

Section 3 Assignment: Which of Columbus' voyages do you find most interesting and why? This assignment could be carried out verbally or in the form of an art project after reading Section 3. One might add: If you had a time machine, which voyage would you most like to be a part of? Why?

Section 4 Activity: Create a list, diagram, or artwork that depicts the different groups of people, creatures, and lands affected by Columbus' discoveries or Search maps to find Columbus-related place names. The latter activity is well suited to this age group and will build their understanding of geography. However, they can also choose the first option. With parental guidance, students can create a basic list, diagram, or artwork that depicts the different groups of people, creatures, and lands affected by Columbus' discoveries. Whether the list is thorough or not, the important point to consider is how different cultures met and how they influenced each other and the landscape. This age group will probably focus most on changes in the New World.

Section 4 Assignment: Extend the rhyme: In 1492, Columbus sailed the ocean blue. Young children develop their language skills through rhymes, so challenge them to find words that rhyme with blue and see if you can come up with any more lines. Allow silly or off topic rhymes but also work together to try to add a line or two that is appropriate to the subject.

Self-Assessment and Reflection: Conduct a short discussion in which the student looks back on the various activities and assignments. Think about:

- Which assignments were difficult (or easy)? Why?

- Was there something that was difficult at first that you can now do more easily?

- How did you overcome any difficulties?

- How is your voyage like Columbus'? How is it different?

Ages 8-10

A summary of tasks for this age group is listed in bold below. This age group can do most of the activities and assignments without major modifications. Assignments should take a range of forms, from written work to role-playing and artwork. Children in this age group should be able to read much of the text with minimal aid. Still, it is good practice to provide different deliveries of the text: some sections can be read independently and others can be read aloud by the student to the parent, or vice versa. It may be necessary to simplify the text or omit more elaborate passages.

Section 1 Assignment: Write a persuasive letter from Columbus to Portugal's King Juan II. Students can prepare a list of important points and then draft a formal letter. They can try one polite and one demanding version of the same exchange.

Section 2 Activity: Practice dead reckoning. This age group should work with plotting 360° courses. They can be introduced to the concept of true versus magnetic compass course and sketch examples to compare how the difference diverges over long distances (depending on one's position on the globe). Discuss other factors that affect the movement of a boat over the sea.

Section 2 Assignment: Make a collage or comic strip depicting Columbus' first journey. Students should create a series of images to represent Columbus' first journey, from finding a royal sponsor to his return with news of his discoveries.

Section 3 Activity: Plot Columbus' trips on a chart along with your own. Define geographic features such as continents, islands, peninsulas, etc. Discuss the idea of the Ocean Sea and look at a modern world chart. Sketch the route of Columbus' trips onto relevant sections of your chart. Do you ever intersect his course? Using our modern knowledge of prevailing winds and currents, examine Columbus' routing. Should he have chosen a different course if he had this knowledge? This exercise will reinforce your own trip in your child's mind as well as reinforce important aspects of history and geography.

Section 3 Assignment: Which of Columbus' voyages do you find most interesting and why? Students should write an essay or create artwork that covers the major points of that voyage and the reasons why it is interesting. They can change "most interesting" to "most adventurous" or "most difficult." If the student had a time machine, which voyage would she most like to be a part of? Why?

Section 4 Activity: Create a list, diagram, or artwork that depicts the different groups of people, creatures, and lands affected by Columbus' discoveries, or search maps to find Columbus-related place names. Students should create a diagram or artwork and refer back to the text, an important study skill. Encourage students to complete a second draft that is neat and clear. Students should consider people and the environment on both sides of the Atlantic.

Section 4 Assignment: Extend the rhyme: In 1492, Columbus sailed the ocean blue. Challenge students to find words that rhyme with blue and see if they can come up with any more lines. Even if they can't make a rhyme, try adding lyrical lines. Try to pinpoint or summarize an important aspect of Columbus' explorations and then apply this to the rhyme.

Self-Assessment and Reflection: Written reflection is appropriate for this age group although students will need prompting to elaborate. Pose questions such as:

- Which assignment did you enjoy the most (or least)? Why?

- Was there something you did incorrectly at first and later did better?

- What advice would you give another student doing the same exercise?

- What resources did you have available to you? Which was the most useful? Why?

- How is your voyage like Columbus'? How is it different?

Ages 10-12

These "oldest" students can work through the challenges in the above assignment in full. Assignments should take a range of forms, from written work to role-playing and artwork. If the student expresses a particular interest or proposes a different activity, follow it by all means! Students ages ten to twelve will be able to read the text independently. Still, it is good practice to provide different deliveries of the text: some sections could be read independently, and others can be read aloud by the student to the parent, or vice versa.

Section 1 Assignment: Write a persuasive letter from Columbus to Portugal's King Juan II. Students in this age group should prepare a list of important points and then draft a formal letter. They should be very thorough in their reasoning and include evidence (in as far as Columbus believed he had evidence) to support their proposals. When listing what Columbus seeks as a reward, be careful lest King Juan II again turn down the proposal!

Section 2 Activity: Practice dead reckoning. Students can learn about true and magnetic compass courses and sketch examples to compare how the difference can diverge over long distances. They can plot exact courses on a chart and consider other factors that affect the movement of a boat over the sea. Very advanced students might enjoy the challenge of factoring leeway, tides, or currents into their chart work.

Section 2 Assignment: Make a collage or comic strip depicting Columbus' first journey. Students should create an extended series of images to represent Columbus' first journey, from finding a royal sponsor to his return with news of his discoveries.

Section 3 Activity: Plot Columbus' trips on a chart along with your own. Help students define geographic features such as continent, island, peninsula, gulf, bay, etc. Discuss the idea of the Ocean Sea and look at a modern world chart. Sketch the route of Columbus' trips onto relevant sections of your chart. Do you ever intersect his course? Using our modern knowledge of prevailing winds and currents, examine Columbus' routing. Should he have chosen a different course? Which sections of his voyages can be considered perfectly routed, according to modern knowledge? This exercise will reinforce your own trip in your child's mind as well as reinforce important aspects of history and geography.

Section 3 Assignment: Which of Columbus' voyages do you find most interesting and why? Students should write a thorough essay or create a well-developed piece of artwork that covers the major points of that voyage and the reasons why it is interesting. Students can change "most interesting" to "most adventurous" or "most difficult." Essay writing should be approached very seriously by this age group. Challenge students to produce a thorough and detailed response, always supporting statements with reasons. Guide them through good essay format, from an introductory statement ("There are many different sides to a historical story...") to supporting statements, and finally a conclusion.

Section 4 Activity: Create a list, diagram, or artwork that depicts the different groups of people, creatures, and lands affected by Columbus' discoveries or Search maps to find Columbus-related place names. Students should create a diagram or artwork and refer back to the text for information, an important study skill. The assignment should consider people and the environment on both sides of the Atlantic. Students should sketch a first draft of their intended format and then complete a more polished second draft. The second activity is simplistic for this age group but is still fun and useful in building a sense of geography.

Section 4 Assignment: Extend the rhyme: In 1492, Columbus sailed the ocean blue. Challenge students to find words that rhyme with *blue* and try to add more lines. Even if they can't make a rhyme, try adding lyrical lines. Try to pinpoint or summarize an important aspect of Columbus' explorations and then apply this to the rhyme.

Self-Assessment and Reflection: Students should make a written statement analyzing their own work.

- Which assignment did you enjoy the most, and why? The least?

- Was there something you did incorrectly at first and later did better?

- Which assignment did you complete best? Why?

- What advice would you give another student?

- What resources did you have available to you? Which was the most useful, and why?

- What do you have in common with explorers like Columbus? What are your differences?

Enrichment

If the many activities and assignments above are not enough for you, consider extending the learning experience in one of the following ways:

- Visit a place related to Columbus and create a photo essay about it. How does the site fit in to what you have learned?

- Research native people of the Caribbean and Americas, or another area of your choice. What were the similarities or differences between the Lucayo, Taino, and Carib groups?

- Follow up on other explorers who sailed in Columbus' wake.

- Study the life of Bartolomé de Las Casas.

- Research the Atlantic slave trade.

- Do a research project focusing on the early European settlers of the Caribbean or another area. What brought them to the New World? What was life like for them?

Resources

Samuel Eliot Morison is one of the leading authorities on Columbus and has written several biographies. The most practical for advanced students is *Christopher Columbus: Mariner*, which is concise yet thorough. Morison re-created parts of Columbus' voyages in sailboats; he examines the historical evidence from the point of view of a sailor. His book was first published in 1942 and has gone through several printings.

Another Columbus enthusiast is Keith Pickering whose easy-to-use website[1] provides a good introduction to the explorer, his voyages, and his means of navigation.

Bartolomé de Las Casas, a priest who argued for better conditions and treatment of native people in the 1500s, could be called the first human rights activist in the New World. A study of his life and work would broaden a student's understanding of the Spanish colonial era: http://www.lascasas.org.

Quotes from Robert H. Fuson. *The Log of Christopher Columbus*. Camden: International Marine, 1987.

About *Lesson Plans Ahoy!*

This chapter is an excerpt from my book *Lesson Plans Ahoy*, which includes detailed instructions for units in science (model the lunar cycle, dissect a fish, and try chemistry), math (graph resource use and study geometry), writing (develop journal, non-fiction, and creative writing skills), history (bring the voyages of Columbus and Captain Cook to life), navigation (compass use, hands-on mapping, and more), and physical education (study heart rate and exercise). All are designed to be fun, practical, and relevant. *Lesson Plans Ahoy* also includes extensive sections on the how-to's of homeschooling on a boat (from choosing a program to designing your own curriculum and keeping students motivated); age-appropriate adaptations for ages 4-12 in detail; tips for cross-curricular links and enrichment; suggested resources to support learning, and materials required (selected for practicality).

---

[1] http://columbuslandfall.com/ccnav/index.shtml

Appendices

Family Cruising: An Interview

We were interviewed by *Women & Cruising* after our first, year-long "seabattical" on topics ranging from challenges to rewards and the details of day to day life on a boat. We hope the answers may inspire others or clarify some practical points for families interested in a longer sailing sojourn.

What was the biggest challenge you faced in getting out there? How did you deal with it?

The biggest challenge for us was simply making the decision to go. At the time, it seemed a gargantuan task to untangle ourselves from our land lives and go to sea. We had the dream but couldn't quite take the leap of faith until we attended a presentation at a boat show and met a couple who had taken six months to cruise the Mediterranean with their infant daughter. That was the straw that broke the reluctant camel's back: if they could do it, so could we.

Once we reached our decision, everything fell into place and we never had second thoughts. Within six months, we were looking at boats. Within a year, we had purchased our 1981 Dufour 35, and a year after that, we set sail. In retrospect, this was an excellent time frame: slow enough to prepare well, but not too far away to lose sight of our goals.

How old were your children when you went cruising? Is there a best age to take children cruising?

Children of all ages have much to gain from life under sail. In addition to enjoying a unique family adventure and seeing new parts of the world, children often develop greater independence and self-confidence than their peers on land. Although our son, Nicky, was very young when we cruised, he still shows the influence in terms of an open mind, genuine curiosity about the world, and an optimistic, positive attitude — *we can do it, fix it, or find it if we work together.*

Our son was three and four during our first "seabbatical." It seemed a perfect age at the time because he wasn't a clueless toddler and not yet in school. Many families cruise with infants and report how easy they find that to be, while others cruising with older children list the benefits, too.

A bonding experience for the whole family

As for older children, I gained an interesting insight from a teenager who had cruised for three years when she was in grades three to five. Her opinion was that while many teenagers would initially miss social contact, they quickly realize what a wonderful life cruising is. Personally, she still pined for a return to the sea and felt the experience had deeply shaped her own life.

It seems there is no perfect age for a child—just the perfect attitude on the part of the parents. If you love sailing and the cruising life, it will rub off on your children. Conversely, if you feel doubts or unease, your children will likely pick up on this and reflect what they sense.

Do you have suggestions for boat features or modifications that are particularly applicable for cruising families?

Taking a child to sea requires basic preparations. For example, we purposely chose a boat with a deep, spacious cockpit. We also made a small ladder so that Nicky could independently access his padded pilot berth with its high sides. Nicky had two life jackets: a self-inflating one for passages and a bulky, orange jacket for wet dinghy rides. Either could be clipped to a tether. The netting we put around the lifelines proved as useful for catching loose toys and tools as setting a boundary for him.

We worked our way up to longer passages just as he did, going from overnight hops to three night passages, then six-day trips, and finally, our Atlantic crossing (twenty-six days from Lanzarote to Antigua). Later, our longest Pacific passage was twenty-eight days and it was easy for all members of the crew.

Is there anything that you wish you had known about cruising as a family before you got started?

Once we had made the decision to go and were preparing for departure, I had few doubts, but from time to time I did wonder what I was getting myself into. It would have been reassuring to know that cruising was the best thing we ever did for ourselves and our son, to know how absolutely privileged we were to live the simple life on the water.

Do you have any advice for families that are considering going cruising?

Our advice is to go, and go now, before some health, financial or family constraint arises and locks your dreams away forever. Your children will enjoy the experience of a lifetime with the people who count most: their parents. Aim for simplicity, not luxury. Your boat doesn't have to be perfect; it just has to be safe, keeping the water out and the people in. Prepare yourself and your boat thoroughly, and then prepare to go with the flow. The close confines of your hull are not a constraint but rather,

107

the vehicle to a limitless world beyond.

Tell us about a typical day at anchor.

During our first three months in the Mediterranean, we never stayed out at anchor for more than a week before going into a marina or a town quay with access to fresh water and shore power/electricity. In the Caribbean, we became much more independent, spending more than five continuous weeks at anchor at a time. (Later, in the Pacific, we stretched that to months at a time.) When we did call in at a marina, we usually couldn't wait to get out again.

What changed? Primarily, it was our improved ability to keep our consumption of fresh water, electricity, fuel and food supplies in line with what we could re-provision/generate without tying up in a marina. We truly enjoy our autonomous little floating home with wind and solar-generated power and the very conscious use of fresh water and electricity—without feeling deprived of any luxury. For us, the peace and beauty of swinging at anchor and jumping off the boat for a swim far outweigh the "conveniences" that marinas offer.

Tell us about a typical day on passage.

On passage, we maintained a regular watch schedule that worked well for us: three or four-hour watches at night and four-hour watches during the day. Our son was too young to take a watch. We adults spent much of our off-watch time sleeping. I learned to prepare things for my son before I went off watch: an accessible snack, drink, and game so that he wouldn't have to disturb me when I really needed my sleep. He was very independent and considerate of our sleeping time, and we were always able to enjoy time together during on-watch times.

One highlight of our Atlantic crossing was the day a whale repeatedly visited us, repeatedly swimming alongside as if to investigate whether *Namani's* hull was one of her kind or not. Nicky was thrilled and spent the following hours studying his cetacean field guide.

Health and Safety: How do you handle...

Keeping kids safe aboard

Before setting off, I worried about storms and illness, all for naught. By sailing along well-established routes in safe seasons and tuning in to forecasts, the worst we ever endured was barely a Force 8, even in the open Atlantic. Away from the germ breeding grounds of school and work, we were never healthier. The only illness any of us suffered was the flu brought by a visitor from North America! Otherwise, we felt safer than at home and freer to enjoy the little things that count.

Our greatest medical incident in a year of sailing occurred when Nicky managed to push a small piece of Lego up his nose. We were on St. Lucia at the time and easily found a doctor who helped clear up the problem, so to speak. Otherwise, our only injuries came from severely stubbing our toes when walking barefoot on deck during the first weeks of our trip. After that, we developed a knack for avoiding the deck hardware.

Caring for the kids in rough weather

When the weather got rough, our son simply put himself to bed in his snug berth and waited it out. After an extended period of time in quiet waters, he often felt seasick on the first day back at sea, but quickly regained his sea legs. As for me, I was sometimes queasy but only truly seasick once in a year; the same holds for my husband.

Education and Fulfillment: How do you handle...

Friendships and social interactions

Our son was the catalyst for several deep friendships with fellow cruisers. In Tunisia, only two months into our trip, we met an American cruising family. Their older son was a year younger than ours, and the boys hit it off instantly (the younger brother was an easy-going baby at the time). We spent a month together in Tunisia and Spain. Our new friends followed the same cruising path we did from the Mediterranean to the Canaries, the Caribbean, and up the U.S. East Coast, although at a slightly different pace. This meant that we joined up on six different occasions over seven months, communicating all the time via SSB radio.

In Gibraltar, we made fast friends with an English family also cruising on a modest budget. We crossed the Atlantic in tandem with them, maintaining daily radio contact, and then stuck together for three months of carefree Caribbean cruising. We have maintained contact with both families ever since, although our three families have settled on three different continents!

Schooling

Because our son was not yet of school age on that first trip, we had great leeway in what we undertook in terms of education. Cruising presents endless teachable moments for the alert parent—from cetacean studies to sea shell classification, lessons on buoyancy and basic physics (kids love hoisting a variety of gear with pulleys), learning about the volcanoes smoking before our very eyes or studying the details of local currency. There is no dearth of learning opportunities at sea or on land.

When Nicky was in the earliest stages of literacy, we helped him keep a journal by allowing him to select a postcard as often as possible (for passages, I bought a few ahead of time, featuring sunsets, turtles, and the like). At first, he would dictate his thoughts to us to write on the card and later, wrote the words himself. We collected the cards in a tin box. This has created a nice visual and written reminder of his many adventures at sea and on land. A sample entry written en route from Ibiza to mainland Spain reads: "We are out at sea. There are giant waves and a sunset and on the other side we see a little more orange. I have a dolphin shirt. We are going to the big part of Spain."

Three years later, we set off on a second trip that took us from Maine to Australia. Our son completed grades two, three, and four in those three years, and it was a priceless experience for us as a family. We based our curriculum on the detailed yearly planner and learner outcomes from his school back at home, but adapted units to our context.

Keeping kids entertained

Keeping a child entertained while at anchor is no issue: there is always a beach, a playground, or an excursion to draw you away from a lazy afternoon on board! At sea, we quickly found that our son was equally easy-going. Before longer passages, I made sure to stash a surprise of some kind for my son–glitter glue, a puzzle, or a mini Lego set. This strategy worked so well that he feverishly looked forward to any major passage! He'd then spend hours happily tinkering below and maintained the ability to entertain himself long after we returned to land.

An adventure in every port

Personal space aboard

Personal space was never an issue even aboard our relatively small thirty-five footer which has one forward cabin, pilot berths in the salon, and one quarter berth aft. Our son was content with his pilot berth while my husband and I took the forward berth or slept on the settees in the salon during passages. During our Atlantic crossing with a friend aboard, everyone had his or her own bunk in the salon or quarter berth. Between the movement of the boat and the fact that at least one person was asleep at any one time, space never seemed to be an issue.

In the Caribbean, we had one friend visit for five weeks and we all treasured the experience. One couple stayed for another fun week. It helps to have easy-going, accommodating friends! We would love to own a forty-footer with an extra guest cabin, but our *Namani* is what we could afford, and we made it work. She truly was our home.

Family back home and their concerns

It was hard on both sets of grandparents to see their little grandson head off to sea, an apparently dangerous venture as far as they were concerned. It did reassure them that we chose to approach our first ocean crossing with an organized flotilla (we joined the Blue Water Rally on its first legs from Gibraltar to Lanzarote and Antigua). After that experience, we gained the confidence to create our next crossing group in a more ad hoc way, teaming up with cruisers we found along the way.

It was very reassuring for our families to be able to receive regular email as we crossed the ocean, using short messages sent via the SSB. Finally, both sides of the family came to visit us aboard the boat and in that way, were able to visualize what we were undertaking more clearly.

Tasks and Chores: How do you handle...

Laundry

Our boat, *Namani*, was very simple with few amenities. I was determined to stretch our budget as far as possible and so we rarely paid for laundry in coin-ops, much less marinas (we usually anchored out for long stretches at a time). Instead, we bucket washed our laundry. In the tropics, you wear very little and jump in the water often, so we didn't feel that our clothes got dirty as quickly as in normal life, but neither did we maintain particularly strict standards.

We learned to make the most of our few marina visits by anchoring nearby the previous night and checking into the marina early. That gave us nearly a full day with running water and power to thoroughly wash everything on board and stock up on supplies. Then we would leave as late as possible the next day.

Clean-up and daily maintenance of the boat

We would periodically spend several days catching up with work on the boat, roughly four to five days of work for every three to five weeks spent cruising. To do so, we would pick a location with good shore-side facilities such as chandlers and hardware stores. For example, we found good facilities in Malta, Almerimar (Spain), Lanzarote (Puerto Calero), Antigua (Jolly Harbor), Grenada (Prickly Bay), Guadeloupe (Pointe-à-Pitre), Saint-Martin (Simpson Bay), and Puerto Rico (Puerto del Rey).

For cleaning while underway, I found household wet-wipes to be indispensable and used grease-cutting wet wipes for the galley.

Feeding the family, nutrition and cooking

Over time, I got to be quite an expert on provisioning and developed a collection of simple "menus" that were practical for underway or in general in our tight galley. We had a refrigerator, but no reliable means to power it, so it took some getting used to provisioning without refrigeration. However, it was entirely worth it not to have to listen to a generator for hours or have another piece of equipment that needed maintenance and repairs.

For long passages, I bought canned chicken and long-life tofu as protein. Eventually, I learned to bake bread. Since we like a multi-grain bread, I would pre-mix the dry ingredients into zip-lock bags before a passage, so all I would have to do was add water and yeast and let it rise. That saved time and the balancing act of measuring on a moving boat.

We didn't follow a particularly healthy diet on long passages like our Atlantic crossing, principally eating canned and dry goods once the fresh produce ran out. We later added sprouts to our repertoire and enjoyed having a crispy fresh ingredient with our meals. Unfortunately, we were not very successful at fishing. Near land, we ate well, buying at local markets or from Caribbean "boat boys" who we generally found to be reliable, patient, and helpful.

What do you like best about cruising (or cruising as a family)?

Markus replied: Something you really only appreciate when you get back to a land-locked life is having experienced nature twenty-four hours a day, every day, while cruising. I came to know when to expect a certain star to rise above the horizon, and got a feel for local weather because I had the time to observe cloud formations developing. Even the somewhat scary experience of being in a lightning storm at sea was something special about our life aboard *Namani*.

One particular memory for me was an overnight passage from Anguilla to Puerto Rico under a full moon—a nice east-to-west downwind run on my birthday. About an hour after the moon moved past directly overhead to slightly ahead, we could literally feel its pull as the tide made our speed over ground pick up by about a knot. It was a beautiful and memorable night in touch with nature.

Another special thing about cruising was getting good at it and doing so as a family. This was something we only became aware of when friends visited or when dockside observers pointed it out to us. Without us noticing at the time, we developed a quiet confidence for many things we had been apprehensive about when we just started, from anchoring in tricky spots, to handling the boat in stronger winds, or docking in tight spaces. More importantly, we did so without losing many words. Soon, it all became a smooth routine.

Nadine's reply: My favorite thing was being able to live life at a pace that was dictated by us or by the weather. We shared a lovely, special time without the artificial stress of the rat race. I loved the fresh air and the magic of lone night watches at sea with my family sound asleep a step away. I enjoyed the way those times allowed my thoughts time to develop and extend. I loved being a partner in a family enterprise with my husband and son.

What do you like least about cruising?

Time seems to smooth over rough patches, so I really can't remember anything significant! Even on one "bad" day in Bequia, I realized how happy I was. I had the flu, I was sad to have parted with dear friends who'd just headed in a different direction, and then I smashed my head against a tree branch. I sat in the sand crying for a minute but at the same moment I realized how good my life was, how this "bad" day was something I would gladly trade for the opportunity to live such a wonderful and rewarding lifestyle.

Why did you go cruising as a family? And how has that panned out so far?

Since I was a teen, day sailing with my father, it was my dream to go cruising and to someday cross an ocean. Luckily, my husband was convinced, too. He grew up without sailing but picked it up quickly and eventually exceeded me as a sailor. We worked our way up by fixing and then sailing a neglected seventeen-footer one summer. Later, we sailed in a vacation flotilla, then chartered with a skipper, and then chartered alone. We also signed on as delivery crew on a yacht from Mallorca to Malta to gain overnight sailing experience.

We went cruising as a family because we wanted to share the experience with our son. Hearing the positive experiences of so many other families gave us confidence in the sanity of our venture. Another factor was my fear of putting off our sailing dreams until retirement. My father dreamed about circumnavigating "someday" but died at age forty-seven from cancer and could not achieve those dreams. Naturally, that left a deep impression on me. I truly believe in the simple message: Go, and go while you can!

Has cruising changed you/your family? How?

I personally found myself positively changed by our family sailing experiences in several ways. I have become more flexible, less uptight. A year at the mercy of unpredictable elements has broken my illusion that I could be master of my universe if I worried enough about it. Now, I go with the flow—a major shift for this type-A control freak. I let the little things go and appreciate what counts: love, health, and good fortune, not to mention kindness to strangers in a strange land.

Before our trip, I would have said that I loved my son but not my role as a mother: the constant demands, the lack of quiet time and space for myself. Was I the only mother to feel this way, I wondered, or the only one to admit it? When we first moved aboard, I struggled with the twenty-four hour togetherness. With time, however, I grew to not only love my son as a person, but to treasure the hours we spent together. Ironically, spending more time with him had the effect of making me want more, rather than wishing for a break. My son was no longer an accessory; he became a fun, loving, eye-opening companion at my side. In this way, I truly feel that I became a better mother during our cruise.

Sailing provides the uncommon opportunity for families to spend long hours together on a daily basis and establish a truly special bond. This is particularly true for children and their fathers. My husband had time for fun and routine pursuits with our son every single day for a year, a priceless experience. My mother-in-law remarked upon it immediately when we returned home and she saw little Nicky resting comfortably in Markus' lap: "This trip has been good for you," she observed warmly. And she was right. Cruising had been a chance for us all to work toward a common goal and thereby deepen our bonds.

Resources for Caribbean Cruising as a Family

The following are titles we recommend for your on-board library, as well as useful Internet sites and social media groups that will help you connect with fellow sailors.

Books

Lesson Plans Ahoy: Hands-On Learning for Sailing Children and Home-Schooling Sailors by Nadine Slavinski. *Lesson Plans Ahoy* includes detailed instructions for units in Science (model the lunar cycle, dissect a fish, and try chemistry), Math (graph resource use and study geometry), Writing (develop journal, non-fiction, and creative writing skills), History (bring the voyages of Columbus and Captain Cook to life), Navigation (compass use, hands-on mapping, and more), and Physical Education (study heart rate and exercise). All are designed to be fun, practical, and relevant. The book also includes extensive sections on the How-To's of homeschooling on a boat (from choosing a program to designing your own curriculum and keeping students motivated); age-appropriate adaptations for ages 4-12 in detail; tips for cross-curricular links and enrichment; suggested resources to support learning, and materials required (selected for practicality). An appendix links the units in the book to national and state curricula of the United States, United Kingdom, Australia, and Canada, so that homeschooling students can keep pace with expectations in their home systems.

Smithsonian Handbooks: An excellent series of compact, well-ilustrated guides. Our favorites are Ian Ridpath's *Stars and Planets*, Mark Carwardine's *Whales, Dolphins, and Porpoises*, and Peter Dance's *Shells*.

The Klutz Guide to the Galaxy by Pat Murphy. This is the book that got our son hooked on stargazing. It comes with a red flashlight and a kit for making a basic telescope.

The Stars: A New Way To See Them by H.A. Rey. In this classic, the creator of *Curious George* re-draws the lines connecting the constellations so they make sense. A great book for all ages.

Websites

Sailkidsed[1] lists many free resources for homeschooling sailors, including recommended books and websites as well as an informative section that describes how different families approach homeschooling

Women & Cruising[2] offers advice, resources, and inspiration for women cruisers. There are post covering sailing with children, conquering your fears, and much more. Take the time to read through the excellent 12 Questions to 12 Sailing Families[3] section.

Family Adventure Podcast[4]. If you're still considering what the scope of your trip will be, you'll find plenty of inspiration and advice on this excellent program. Many of the adventuresome families interviewed on the podcast are sailors.

Caribbean Safety and Security Net[5] has unfortunately discontinued their daily radio net but continued to post important bulletins to the website.

---

[1] http://www.sailkidsed.net
[2] http://womenandcruising.com/
[3] http://womenandcruising.com/sailing-families.htm
[4] http://www.familyadventurepodcast.com/
[5] https://www.safetyandsecuritynet.com/

Chris Parker's Marine Weather Center[1] is a website and radio service that covers the Caribbean and US East Coast. His daily weather reports are free, and you can subscribe to his individualized services for a fee.

Facebook Groups

Kids4Sail is a Facebook group for cruising families who are currently living or preparing to live aboard or cruise. A group map is available to track members and their locations to use as a tool for meeting up and sharing information.

Women Who Sail is another Facebook group where women who love boats can come together and connect. It is a place to share questions, celebrations, rants, and comments about the boating life.

---

[1] https://www.mwxc.com/

About the Author

Nadine Slavinski is a teacher, writer, and erstwhile archaeologist with a penchant for blue horizons. She holds a Master's of Education from Harvard University and has been teaching in international schools since 1996. Her son Nicky crossed his first ocean at age four and later completed grades two, three, and four while sailing the Pacific Ocean aboard *Namani*.

Visit Nadine's website *www.nslavinski.com* to find interesting and informative blog posts, links, and resources. That's also where you can contact her or sign up to receive updates on new content and releases. Her travel blog is at *www.namaniatsea.org*.

Also by Nadine Slavinski:

- *Lesson Plans Ahoy! Hands-on Learning for Sailing Children and Home-Schooling Sailors*

- *Lesson Plans To Go: Hands-on Learning for Active and Home-Schooling Families*

- *Pacific Crossing Notes: a Sailor's Guide to the Coconut Milk Run*

Please consider leaving a review of this book at the store you purchased it from. Not only do reviews help other readers judge a book, they also help the title appear more often in Internet searches and thus find interested readers. This is especially important to niche publications like this, so please do write a review, no matter how brief. Thank you!

Also by Nadine Slavinski

The Silver Spider, a sea adventure novel.

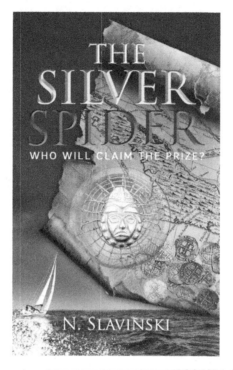

A mountain of treasure in Panama: whose will it be?

In 1667, a Spanish soldier makes a startling discovery. A vast treasure – or a curse? Two centuries later, Charlie Parker, engineer and adventurer, voyages to Central America to build the Panama Canal – and engage in a few extracurricular activities in his spare time.

Two modern-day sailors get more adventure than they bargained for when they unravel a cryptic tangle of clues. Have they inherited incredible riches – or just big trouble?

Pieces of Eight. A silver spider. Plotting pirates. Scheming cartels. A treasure map without an X. Who will claim the prize?

Made in United States
North Haven, CT
04 November 2022

26279579R00075